CURLING ROCKS!

JOHN CULLEN

CURLING ROCKS!

CHRONICLES OF THE ROARING GAME

Douglas & McIntyre

2 3 4 5 6 — 30 29 28 27 26

Douglas and McIntyre (2013) Ltd.
P.O. Box 219, Madeira Park, BC, V0N 2H0
www.douglas-mcintyre.com

Edited by Charlie Demers
Cover illustration by Heidi Berton
Illustrations by Alyssa Hirose
Text design by Libris Simas Ferraz / Onça Publishing
Printed and bound in Canada
Printed on 100% recycled paper

Canada Council for the Arts
Conseil des arts du Canada

Douglas and McIntyre acknowledges the support of the Canada Council for the Arts, the Government of Canada, and the Province of British Columbia through the BC Arts Council.

Library and Archives Canada Cataloguing in Publication

Title: Curling rocks! : chronicles of the roaring game / John Cullen.
Names: Cullen, John (Curler), author.
Identifiers: Canadiana (print) 20250239183 | Canadiana (ebook) 20250239221 | ISBN 9781771624558 (softcover) | ISBN 9781771624565 (EPUB)
Subjects: LCSH: Curling. | LCSH: Curling—Canada.
Classification: LCC GV845 .C85 2025 | DDC 796.964—dc23

For Becca,
who encourages all my dumb ideas

CONTENTS

INTRODUCTION

JUST ANOTHER NASHVILLE CURLING STORY...

I'm sitting at a bar in Nashville, Tennessee. And it's not just any bar; it's a *curling* bar. It is both an odd place for such an establishment and an odd place for a book about curling to start, but curling is no longer just your grandfather's Canadian curio. Curling isn't only an excuse for small-town Canadians to gather in the wintertime, getting out of the −20 cold and into a much warmer place, like the −2 of a curling club, gossiping about the neighbours who don't curl, and bringing home dusty old trophies with auras of cigarette smoke and stale beer. Curling is not a sport for the out-of-shape armchair athlete who dreams of making the Olympics but doesn't want to put in the requisite time or effort to do so, for comedians and the common man alike to make fun of. This curling bar that I'm sitting in—which, by the way, is owned by two-time Pro Bowl NFL quarterback Marc

Bulger—is a sign that things are changing for the sport, and they're changing rapidly, and for the better.

I'm here at Tee Line—named after the line in curling that bisects the button and the centre line (we'll get to that later)—for the first-ever Grand Slam of Curling All-Star Game. It's an indication of the sport's growth: curling is now popular enough not only to attract fans to an all-star game, but also to set that game at a bar in the American South. The Grand Slams were recently purchased by The Curling Group, an organization that sees a big opportunity for curling in the modern sports landscape, where sports that were previously thought to be niche, like disc golf and darts, are gaining a huge foothold in the market. Their plan to expose the sport to new audiences involves things like this all-star game, bringing 12 of the best curlers in the world—from places like Switzerland and Sweden and Scotland—to Nashville to play a game against each other, take part in a skills competition, a pro-am game, and just generally do things that other, larger sports have been doing for a long time. Curling is growing up, and it's the story of four NFLers that might have started it all.

It all begins with Jared Allen. If you're a football fan, particularly a Minnesota-loving one, you'll know who Jared Allen is. But in the event that you don't, he was a defensive end in the NFL for 12 seasons. He was a four-time First Team All-Pro and a five-time Pro Bowler; he led the NFL in sacks twice, and he is in the Minnesota Vikings' Ring of Honor and was named one of the 50 greatest Vikings in 2010. He was also elected to the Pro Football Hall of Fame in 2025. If you have never heard of any of *that*, you may remember him as the NFL player who absolutely plowed Johnny Knoxville in *Jackass 3*. He's 6'6", weighs 255 pounds, and is one hell of an athlete. And once his NFL playing career was finished, he did what a lot of others have done: he saw curling on TV, figured he could do it, and decided it was an easy pathway to making the Olympics, on a dare from some buddies.

For a lot of people, the story might have ended there. But not for Jared. He had the competitive drive of one of the best athletes in the world, more than enough money to support his dream, and, all of a sudden, a lot of free time. Instead of directly appealing his case to the curling world and finding out what resources it might have for a defensive end turned curler, he figured he should just ask some of his football-athlete friends to join him. If, after playing one of the toughest pro sports on earth, you believe that curling would be easy for you, then you might also conclude that three more of you would make the strongest team possible. And so it was that Jared Allen started showing up at curling events with Michael Roos, a First-Team All-Pro offensive tackle; Keith Bulluck, a two-time First-Team All-Pro linebacker; and the aforementioned Marc Bulger. It did not go well.

After going winless through a handful of events in the first few years, Bulluck and Roos fell off the program, realizing that curling might be a lot harder than they had imagined. But Allen and Bulger's history in the NFL caught the eye of USA Curling, which matched them up with some veterans who had won US titles before, curlers who could teach the football guys a thing or two about playing the game at its highest level.

Allen is still chasing that dream. He's been to the US National Championships several times, as recently as 2024, and has won more than his share of games there over the years, including one over 2018 Olympic gold medallist John Shuster. His ultimate goal of making the Olympics hasn't been reached yet, and it looks like his best path to doing so might be to improve enough to become the alternate for a more established tour team, but he continues to chase that dream, and to be frank about how much he loves the sport. He loves it so much, in fact, that he became one of the early investors in The Curling Group, and now owns part of the company that is steering curling in a new direction.

As for Bulger, he eventually fell back from playing the game competitively, after never reaching the heights Allen had and never playing at the US National Championships. But he really loved the game, and he loved the family aspect of it: it was a game that kids could play with their parents, where the injury risk was low, particularly compared with football. Although the usual path to learning curling, especially for Canadians, is through either a school program or a junior program at their local curling club, because their parents play, Bulger thought starting a club somewhere that knows nothing about curling, like Nashville, might be prohibitive. And so Tee Line was born, after Bulger saw what Topgolf had done for the game of golf and Brooklyn Bowl had done for bowling. He thought this approach could easily work for curling too. He converted an old warehouse in West Nashville into a bar that serves drinks and food, with four bowling lanes and three curling sheets. It's an accessible way for people to try the sport we all love, and as I'm typing these words and taking it all in, I'll be honest with you: it's a beautiful spot. Every curling fan should come here at least once. It's something unique for our sport—a sport that has lacked new ideas and viewpoints for a long time, a sport where most of the decisions have been made by white Canadians over 60 sitting in a boardroom.

And that is how I came to write this book (not because the older white people in the boardroom assigned me, but because I want to capture some of those new perspectives). Although I didn't necessarily imagine myself starting it in Nashville, Tennessee, I know this sport has been trending in a different direction for the last decade or so. Curling is getting younger, it's getting more professional, and more and more people each year are discovering what makes it so special. It's the most popular sport during the Winter Olympics; the Grand Slams are expanding all the time and to new areas of the globe; new countries are constantly joining World Curling all the time.[1] You can even create a podcast about curling that goes to No. 1 in Canada and the top 10 in a number of countries and wins prestigious podcasting awards. Seriously, I know a guy.

I love this sport, and I love writing about this sport, and for whatever reason, we just don't have that many books about this sport. So I wanted to write one. But I didn't want to write one that was strictly informative or was just a biography of a curler. I wanted to write the type of curling book I wanted to read, one that included stuff about the sport's awful history with fashion, or about which team would be the best if you could only make it up of players who have the same first name, or about losses so crippling you want to quit the sport. Seriously, I know a guy.

So here we are. I hope you enjoy it. But first, seeing as I'm in Nashville, let me sing a little love song. A song about a young Ontario boy's first love triangle... on ice.

---

1 World Curling now counts over 70 member associations from countries around the world—countries you'd never expect to have curling teams, from tropical locales like Puerto Rico and Jamaica to tiny nations like Andorra and Liechtenstein. Even African nations are getting in the mix, with Kenya and Nigeria both boasting teams.

CHAPTER 1

TRADING HOCKEY FOR CURLING

A Canadian Love Story

I was born in southern Ontario in 1985, with skates on. Now, of course, that's just me exaggerating for effect (the English teacher half of me would tell you that in the business we call this "hyperbole"), but it really isn't all that far from the truth. My dad played hockey his entire life, just like his dad did, just like my uncles did, and my cousins did, and, of course, I did. I received my first hockey stick before I was even old enough to hold it. I was destined to be a hockey player, but I couldn't have known at that time that hockey wouldn't become my favourite sport, or the sport I was best at. I couldn't have known it wouldn't even be my favourite sport played on ice. Curling was coming for me, a 42-pound rock hurled at my back, just waiting to catch up to me, waiting for me to hear its roar, like a clumsy polar bear in an extremely slow and slippery chase that lasted until I was 13 years old and I succumbed to the game's sleepy brilliance. Until I turned 13, though, I had hockey to take care of.

One of my family's earliest and most favoured photographs of me is at two years old, shooting a hockey puck into a net in my parent's basement laundry room. I'm wearing a mismatched yellow sweater and green corduroys, my hair slicked down like an old hockey card from the 1950s, a smile on my face that suggests that I know, even at two years of age, that I'm going to be a professional hockey player. You know how inevitably, when NHL stars make it big, we get shown photos and videos of them as kids, looking thrilled with themselves, as though they somehow knew even at that age that they were destined for stardom? That's how I look in that photo. I was never a star, and I would give up on hockey just 10 years later, but in that fleeting moment, anything was possible.

I did not get my first pair of skates at birth, but I got them at age three: a pair of Lange skates that look like something you'd find in a museum today. One of the unfortunate parts of turning 39 is recognizing that things you owned three decades ago could easily qualify for display to bored elementary school students, and even reading about Lange skates now makes me surprised I can still walk without assistance. From the website Ice Hockey Skate Collection:

> A major player in hockey skates during the 1970s were Lange. Lange skates were an outgrowth of their plastic ski boots that had foam liners. The Garcia Company bought out Lange in the early '70s but continued development and marketing of Lange throughout the '70s and early '80s. Phil Esposito endorsed and used Lange skates. They went out of favour due to their weight, and frankly, looks, but for a lot of players, looks weren't everything as they were very comfortable to wear and offered more protection than traditional skates.[1]

I just reread that paragraph and passed out. They were terrible, gaudy, plastic skates, but they were mine and I took to skating right away. Hockey? Less so. In typical Ontario fashion, my parents put me into actual, organized hockey at the age of four. Seems bizarre to think that there would be actual leagues, with referees and jerseys and coaches, at the age of four, but there I was in my red "Ontario Tree Fruits" jersey and equipment my parents had bought at a swap meet, deathly afraid of the buzzer. Yeah, I spent most of the first year telling my parents I didn't want to play hockey because

1 "Lange Ice Skates," Ice Hockey Skate Collection, www.iceskatehistory.co.uk/lange.

the buzzer was too loud. It's probably why I grew up hating electronic dance music. But hockey found a way to endure.

It's very easy to romanticize sports. I think when you grow up in a small town that is so heavily influenced by sport culture, you feel like you're growing up in a world no one else can understand. I suppose it probably isn't all that hard to understand, since every sport seems to have its stories of players that emerged from literally nothing, after being born with a soccer ball at their feet or a baseball bat in their hands. The story of southern Ontario's relationship with hockey is one that is written in countless spots around the globe, the same passions squeezing out of different sports. And with due respect to all the little pitchers and midfielders around the globe, my childhood was entirely composed of hockey. We played road hockey every day after school. We skated on the ravine behind my house, sometimes bringing sticks and pucks, sometimes just skating its two-or-so-kilometre length until it got too dark to see, and then sometimes even after that. We collected hockey cards and hockey pogs and hockey shirts and hats and magazines and programs and ticket stubs. It was, without hyperbole (there's that word again), my entire life.

To put it into perhaps a clearer context that isn't just listing a very normal childhood obsession, I grew up in a township about an hour outside of Toronto (give or take a parking lot-sized traffic jam), where the population was eighteen thousand between the four towns combined. We had our own hockey rink, which somehow wasn't enough. Most of my childhood was spent in the midst of a fundraising campaign to build a second ice hockey pad, because they were running out of ice times for our single ice pad. *In a town of eighteen thousand.* That seems almost impossible to imagine, but it was presented as a dire need, with folks going so far as to place a giant thermometer in the middle of town, updating the money that had been donated to the cause. The second ice pad got built just before we moved. I just looked at pictures of the old rink in order to write this up, and I cried.

Off the ice rink, I went to gifted school. This information isn't really that important, and although the word *gifted* used to be synonymous with *smart*, it has gained new life in the last few years as a synonym for *damaged*, and I'm not here to speculate about how damaged I am. That said, I'm also investing a lot of my time in writing a book about curling, so... reader's choice. This information is only important insofar as it affected my hockey playing career in two ways.

First, I didn't go to the same school as anyone I played with. My old township borders up against Newmarket, Ontario, a much larger suburb of Toronto and one that's grown in population by twenty-five thousand since I left in 1999. It's the home of NHL superstar Connor McDavid and many, many, many strip malls. And a giant shopping mall too—the Upper Canada Mall—which still exists as a focal point of the city, demonstrating suburban Toronto's emotional growth since I left. Being gifted/damaged, I went to a "magnet school," where all the gifted children from the area were gathered into a single class. My school was 15 minutes away by car and 60 by the short bus I rode every day, for which I was the first pick-up and last drop-off. As you can imagine, not going to school with and, thus, not really being friends with the guys you played hockey with was an issue. (Also, if you're the gifted kid sticking out on your hockey team, try not to say "thus.")

And second, true to gifted-kid form, I wore glasses from the age of six, and immediately my retinas degenerated to the point where I needed them at all waking hours, even while playing contact sports. As you can imagine, they needed some security while I played, so I wore a rainbow-coloured "sports strap" that wrapped around both arms of the glasses and secured them tightly to the back of my neck. The rainbow-colored strap came out of the back of my hockey helmet.

What I'm trying to say here is that I was a huge loser. I think people have a stock picture in their mind of a "hockey player": some frat boy–looking, square-jawed man with improbably stringy hair and a shorthand version of every word in the English language. But no, I was the shortest and skinniest kid on the team, who wore glasses with a rainbow sports strap and got lightning bolts and his hockey number shaved into the side and back of his head, for some reason that I refuse to reach back into the deepest recesses of my mind to understand.

But... I was good. I wasn't "this kid is obviously going to make it" good, but I was good. I played on multiple rep teams, frequently captaining them and leading them in scoring, and while I hold no delusions of grandeur about my abilities relative to actually good hockey players, I was good.

I think I was good at hockey both because of the aforementioned upbringing and also just because, well, I had to be, because that's just what was expected of you as the hockey child of a hockey dad. We had a system, my dad and I, from the time I was about seven years old: if I played well in the game, my father would buy me a pop and a bag of chips, and he would carry my hockey bag to the car. If I did not play well, I would get no treats and I would have to carry my own bag, which, from the ages of seven to nine, was the same size as me (and probably pretty close in weight too). We would then proceed to argue in the car about what I could have done better or why I wasted his time driving 30 minutes to this game only to play poorly and not seem all that interested. I don't have kids of my own yet, but it's something I'm imagining I'll understand better once I do.

I'm sure you're reading this and thinking, "But John, this is a book about curling. Why are you talking about hockey so much?" The reality is that in Canada, we curlers have often played second fiddle to hockey. And not second fiddle in the way that second violin is seated directly beside first violin in an orchestra. If hockey is first violin, we are somewhere backstage, playing along to the same songs, but no one can hear us. That is changing. Curling is becoming a force to be reckoned with, both in this country and worldwide. But I think the story for so many of us Canadians while growing up was that push-and-pull relationship we had with hockey. If you didn't play hockey, you were already kind of a loser. But if you skipped out on the chance to play hockey to play curling? Oh boy, that was something else entirely.

I know, because I lived it.

My story in curling can't exist without hockey, but I hope one day we can get to a place where a Canadian kid tells their story of curling without hockey in the background. I think we can, and I think we will.

But if we flash back to 1998, being good at curling wasn't even on my radar, until something happened that altered my athletic trajectory forever. When I was attending that gifted program, my school offered a program they called "electives," which in hindsight was one of the more beautifully crafted elementary school programs I've ever heard of, and to this day I have yet to meet anyone who got to do the same thing, other than people I went to school with. Here's how it worked: for four Fridays out of the school's calendar year, regular classes were completely abandoned, and you could choose a morning and an afternoon activity to do with one of the teachers in the school. Each teacher was bound to present the school's administration with a program. It could be a full-day program that required travel, like skiing/snowboarding/snowshoeing, but most were a half-day long, and they were eclectic. You could make a stuffed animal with Mrs. Skinner. You could play tennis with Mr. Lozinski. You could go to circus school with Mr. Peck. It was a pretty amazing program both ways: it was a unique opportunity for a student to try something they were unfamiliar with or get better at something they already liked, and to work with a staff member they never really had before, or see them in a new, more casual light. And it was a really cool opportunity for a teacher to share their love of a hobby with students. As a teacher now, I would love to have the excuse to do this with my students. Luckily for me, a teacher at my school loved curling.

I wish I could remember which teacher it was who took us, but I don't. I just remember what they gave me. I didn't know much about curling other than what I had seen on TSN—watching the men's and women's national championships during the February and March weekdays when you were home sick with your yearly cold was a rite of passage for Canadian youth—but I knew enough to know that it was intriguing to me, even if I barely understood the rules or why anyone would play it. And for two afternoons in 1998, I got to try curling, and it was *fun*.

Stepping onto the ice for the first time was one of coolest feelings ever, one I can still remember in very vivid detail. This was mostly because, for kids growing up in Ontario, one of the prime recess activities in winter was to find the ice patches that had formed overnight and slide on them, one end to the other, risking severe injury and rushing to do it before the custodian could sand them down and prevent said fun. Sometimes you'd get lucky and have an entire morning recess before they got sanded, and any time kids had 15 minutes with an ice patch, you ended up with games of chicken, two or more kids sliding at each other from opposite ends and slamming into each other with abandon. This is a long way of telling you that when you go curling for the first time, you are not disallowed but, in fact, *encouraged* to slide on the ice—with a plastic device strapped to your shoe to make you go faster, no less—and there's no adult around who is going to sand it down. I thought I'd died and gone to heaven.

As I learned the little bit about the game I could glean from my roughly five hours with it, I knew I had to try it on a more serious basis. These two afternoons were not enough. Luckily for me, the junior program at the York Curling Club ran on Sunday mornings, a time when I didn't have hockey, ever. So there was no conflict there, other than the fact that my dad didn't want to drive me to the club on Sundays. He said it was something about being too tired after a long workweek, but I think it's far more likely he couldn't imagine his own son playing hockey one day and curling the next. One thing he did appreciate, however, was that the registration fee for the entire curling season was *fifty dollars*. Even adjusting for late-'90s inflation, any parent who knows anything about sports or life, or has just drawn a breath, knows that being able to commit their kid to a sport for an entire year for $50 is akin to pulling $500 out of a scratch-and-win. The parental lottery shone fondly on parents of kids who were nerdy enough and yet confident enough to own that nerdiness and hit the curling ice. Fortunately, my mom was always willing to drive.

And so it was that in my last year in Ontario, I played on two hockey teams and one curling team, spending roughly four nights a week on some sort of ice surface. Curling appealed to me in a way that no other sport had. Did I mention I was a member of the chess club? It feels like that fact has probably permeated your subconscious as you worked your way through this chapter anyway, but yeah. I loved chess. The idea that I could continue to play a sport on ice, in winter, that was nonviolent yet still super physical, full of finesse and aggression, and full of characters like me, and that sport was also described as "chess on ice"? I was all the way in before I even started.

Then we moved to British Columbia. A cross-country move when you're 13 is a lot to handle, but it was something my family approached with care—my dad had the option to transfer but could've opted not to—and my parents decided it was the best move for us. Twenty-two years later, I can confidently say this is an indisputable fact, but at the time, even though I knew I wasn't leaving a lot behind, it was a lot to process, especially when it came to hockey. The politics of minor hockey are tough, and even though I felt like an outsider in a lot of ways, it was still a minor hockey association I had grown up in and gotten to know well. Now I was leaving that behind. And while I didn't know it at the time, I wasn't just leaving that hockey association. I was leaving hockey behind too.

We packed our bags and moved across the country on August 31, 1999, a day that was chosen for two reasons: the first, and more practical, was so that my sister and I could start school on time. But the second was so that I would be able to make rep hockey tryouts. While we packed up most of our belongings onto two moving trucks that were bound to arrive when we took possession of our house in mid-September, we paid extra money to put my hockey equipment and sticks on a plane so that I could make it to hockey tryouts on September 2.

I don't need to belabour the point, but let's just say this strategy did not work. It turns out that for a kid who is used to playing hockey all the time, taking a summer off from the game while moving across the country, then attending hockey tryouts for a brand-new association two days after you land, is not a great set of blueprints to success. Having been cut from all three rep teams after one tryout, I decided that I'd had enough of hockey and it was time to move on. It was time to fully embrace a fact that I had probably known for a year but was now ready to wrap my whole heart around: I was a curler.

I can make excuses and say that if I had been given a fairer shake, things would've turned out differently, but the reality was, I was finished with hockey. The long drives, the hits, the verbal abuse, the culture of the game. Even though I was someone who, at the age of three, could identify all of the NHL teams by their logo and who had probably played somewhere north of five hundred games of organized hockey from age four to fourteen, I never really missed it once I left. I had found my new home, and it was right next door to the hockey rink in White Rock, BC, that I would've played at. It was called Peace Arch Curling Club, and my dad did agree to drive me there, so long as he didn't have to watch the games.

I wish I could tell you that there was some perfect moment in time when I fell in love with the game, a "TSN Turning Point," if you will. But there wasn't one moment.

I truly think that all it took was time—time spent with the game of curling, with its gentle nudges, its collection of big moments wrapped up inside what appeared to be a small game. Maybe it was something as simple as noticing that everyone who curled looked like me. I'm not sure I had enough awareness of my own body or general stand-against-the-wallness to understand and to recognize that these were my people. But there they were: poorly clothed, with jackets and pants sagging off, glasses fogging up with the intensity of the games, talking to each other like every discussion about strategy was dismantling a hastily put-together bomb—hastily assembled, quick to explode. Maybe it was as simple as a lack of violence; the only violent part of curling emerged from its collection of lawyers, mill workers, and sales reps who make up the game's professional players screaming at each other things like "*Hurry hard!*" and "*Right off!*" But once I did fall for it, I fell for it hard.

Throughout this book, my love for curling will become apparent in ways that I can't describe just by comparing it with hockey, and lots of people spend lots of time comparing curling with hockey anyway. If the fabric of our nation were a quilt, those two squares are beside each other, and they're tough to pull apart. But curling did pull itself away from hockey for me, to become a game that I deeply appreciated on all levels, not just as a spectator, but as a player, media commentator,

SKATE RETURN
PUCK

and now author. Curling is a social game, and this is a social book: I hope its chapters meet you where you are, whether that's beside the fire on a cold day or squeezing in a chapter before bed after a rough day or in a curling club lounge, pounding a few back with your teammates and commiserating over a loss.

This book is not just for the die-hard curler or curling fan, but for anyone who has been curious about this game and its broad cast of characters—for anyone who has wished someone might invite them into this world that, I'll admit, seems complicated when you just switch on the television and try to watch a game.

For those already in the world, I hope the book stirs up feelings about how much the game means to all of us, or, at the very least, sparks debate among you and your teammates over a post-Tuesday-night club game. And let's face it: curling is inherently a pretty funny sport. So I hope it makes you laugh too.

I'd write "Hurry hard" here as a sign-off, but since I was usually the lead who would accidentally slip guards into the house, instead I'll say "Whoa, take it easy." It's time to explore the world's most beautiful sport, together.

CHAPTER 2

WHAT IS CURLING? BABY DON'T HURT ME

Now that you know how I fell in love with curling, you're probably thinking: What the hell is curling, anyway? Well, it's really simple: it's like shuffleboard, but with lots of screaming. It's like bocce, if people ran out with small lawnmowers to treat the grass as the ball was in motion. It's like hockey, except instead of a puck there's a rock, and instead of a stick there's a broom, and instead of a skate there's a shoe with Teflon or stainless steel attached to the bottom of it.

Actually, it's unique, and while there's a temptation to compare it to other sports in an attempt to explain it, curling is older than most sports. In fact, it's one of the oldest sports known to man.

Although the exact date and origin of curling are unknown, there is quite a bit of evidence that the game, at least in some form, was being played as early as the 16th century. A curling "stone"—one that looked a lot like a random stone pulled from some riverbed or forest floor, and not like the polished granite you see today—was excavated from an old pond in Dunblane, Scotland, and it had the date 1511 inscribed on it. Even if you have a hard time wrapping your head around the fact that curling is older than Shakespeare, there's more.

Pieter Bruegel the Elder, a Flemish painter renowned for his work throughout the Dutch Renaissance, has roughly 40 surviving works. Two of those works, "Winter Landscape with a Bird Trap" and "The Hunters in the Snow," depict curling. Both are dated 1565. As far as we can tell, Pieter never set foot in Scotland and spent most of his life in what is now known as the Netherlands. It's likely proof that not only did curling exist in the 16th century, but its existence spread throughout Europe. Much like today, the Scots and the Low Countries connected on golf and, it would appear, also on curling, or at least some version of it.

If you're not a visual learner and you prefer your evidence in writing, we don't have to travel too far along the timeline to find it. Scottish poet Henry Adamson is credited with the first mention of curling in writing, in 1620. Writing about the passing of a friend in *The Muses Threnodie, or, Mirthfull Mournings, on the Death of Master Gall*, Adamson remarks that Master Gall was "much given to pastime," including "golf, archerie, and curling," and that his house contained "his hats, his hoods, his bels, his bones; his allay bowles and curling stones."

Given that many people first find curling while flipping through the channels on TV and are immediately drawn in by the sport as a mere curiosity, it is funny to consider that it predates the vast majority of sports we currently play and enjoy. What started on the frozen ponds and lochs of Scotland was brought over to Canada by Scottish immigrants, and in fact the oldest active sports club in North America is the Royal Montreal Curling Club, founded in 1807. The game has deep roots in Canada, but it is also currently played in many countries across the world, with a quick glance at the top 25 rankings in the sport showing representative countries in Europe, Asia, and North America. The game is even beginning to bleed into Africa and South America, with teams from Guyana and Nigeria competing at the most recent Pan Continental Curling Championships.

So what is the game, exactly? We know it's old. Centuries old. We know it has over 1.5 million active players, and it has hundreds of millions of fans, as evidenced by the fact that in every Winter Olympics it ranks among the top sports searched for and talked about on various social media platforms. That doesn't mean most people understand it, though. For a game whose goal is ultimately as simple as "push a stone down a sheet of ice toward a stationary target," there's a lot going on. So let me break it down for you. For those of you who are already curling aficionados, you may feel free either to skip this section or to read it in a spirit of skeptical judgment as to whether I'm explaining it right (some of you are already wondering if I meant "*skip* this section" as a pun).

I'm going to start by assuming you do not care how long the ice sheet is, or how wide it is, or how far the hog line is from the hack. Let's start with what you do care about, and get ready to have your mind blown: everyone both throws and sweeps. There is a not a designated thrower or a designated sweeper. Here are some ways I have been asked this question over the years:

"Are you the guy who throws the thing or the guy who sweeps the thing?"

"Which one of the two things do you do? The... pushing? Or the brushy whatever?"

Or my personal favourite: "Do you do the slide thing or are you the guy who chases after the thing with the stick?"

A curling game generally consists of either eight or ten *ends*. Let's not complicate it: an end is like an inning in baseball. Scoring occurs after the last rock is thrown in each end. Rocks are thrown at the bullseye or target (we call it *the house*) at the opposite end of the sheet.[1] Each team throws eight stones per end, alternating. Once

1 Fine, fine, math nerds: a curling sheet is roughly 150 feet long, and roughly 15.5 feet wide. This can obviously vary based on conditions and surface area in curling clubs.

that last rock comes to rest, whichever team has their rock sitting closest to the centre of the house scores a point. If the next closest rock to the centre belongs to that same team, they score another point. They will keep scoring points in this fashion until the next closest rock belongs to their opponent. To wit, if there is one red rock right in the centre, and a yellow rock sitting next to it, and then *five* other red rocks in the house, red still only scores one. Only one team can score per end. For our visual learners:

A curling team consists of four members. There are eight rocks per team that are thrown in each end, so even our most math-challenged readers can probably intuit that each player throws two rocks each end. When a rock is thrown, two of the thrower's teammates will be there to sweep the rock (we'll get to that in a second), and the fourth teammate will be at the other end of the ice. That is usually the player we call the *skip* (there, now everyone can enjoy the possible pun equally). The skip is the person in charge of strategy for the team. They tell their teammates which shots to play, and they also give their teammates a guideline for where to aim their rocks as they're throwing. Quick, here are all the curling positions:

Lead: As the name suggests, leads throw the first two stones in an end. They typically throw *draw shots*, which are intended to end up in the field of play, and not designed to remove an opponent's stone. After they are done, they'll sweep the remaining six rocks in an end. Leads also tend to be the most intelligent, best-looking, and coolest members of a curling team. Apropos of nothing, I played lead for most of my career.

Second: After the lead, the second throws their team's next two stones. Seconds are typically known for their *takeout* ability. A takeout is a shot that is designed to remove an opponent's stone. Chances are good that if you've seen curling highlights on TV, you've seen a takeout. Like the lead, when they are not throwing, they are sweeping the remaining six stones for their team.

Third: The third has to do it all. Throwing the next two stones after the second, they have to be good at both draws and takeouts. They have to sweep the rocks delivered by the lead and the second. But they also take over the skip's strategic/ice-reading duties when the skip is throwing. They're busy. Typically, the third is the most talented member of a curling team.

Skip: The Big Kahuna. Or, I guess, since this is a Canadian and Scottish sport, the Big Caledonia. The skip doesn't sweep, but instead, for the first six rocks of the end, calls the game. They tell their teammates which shots to throw and how to throw them, typically using their broom as a target. And then they throw the two most important rocks of the end, the last two. They most directly impact who scores in an end, they have the most pressure on their backs, and they have to be really good, or your team won't be. Think of a quarterback in football: cerebral, physical, and in control of their team's destiny. Skips are so important to the team that we name the team after them. If your skip is Brad Gushue, your team is called Team Gushue. No team names here. Just the skips' last names. Imagine that in other sports. Though, honestly, the New England Bradys does have a certain ring to it.

Teams will either flip a coin or compete in a shootout before the game to determine who starts the game with the advantage of throwing the last rock in the first end, an advantage we call the *hammer*. No one is quite sure how that became the term for it, but there's a non-zero chance it's a reference to Thor's hammer. And just when you thought curlers were uncool nerds. Whichever team scores in an end, the opposition will receive the hammer in the next end. So your basic goal with the hammer is to score two or more points, and your goal without the hammer is to force your opponent to score only 1, as it's the cheapest way to get the hammer back and give yourself a chance to score two or more again.

If you have the hammer and your opposition scores any number of points, that is called a *steal*. Damn, maybe curlers are even cooler than I thought. In that instance, the team with the hammer retains it through the next end. If neither team scores, that is called a blank, and the team with the hammer retains it through the next end. Often, if a team with the hammer has an opportunity to remove all the remaining stones in the house when there isn't a better option to score multiple points, they will do just that. And that's it! You now know everything there is to know about curling. Oh wait. I didn't talk about sweeping at all. Oh crap.

CHAPTER 3

NO SWEEP TILL BROOKLYN

Hurry hard! Chances are good that if you know nothing else about curling, you know about two things: the yelling and the sweeping (it really is the only sport modelled on a loveless medieval Scottish marriage). It's fitting that those two things go hand in hand, and it's not a surprise that whenever you take anyone out curling for the first time, they're probably most excited for the yelling part. And the post-game beers. But ignore the sweeping at your peril!

Curlers have had to navigate through decades—nay, centuries—of sweeping jokes. We'd make great housekeepers. Our kitchen floors must be the cleanest in Canada. Even the one mainstream curling movie ever made reached for a joke about it in its title: *Men with Brooms*. As though that was a revolutionary concept. No one really knows what the sweeping does exactly, and when I say that, I'm not patronizing any casual curling fans reading this book. We don't really know either.

Actually, curling mysteries abound. We haven't exactly figured out why the rocks curl. There are physics people far smarter than me who have tackled and are currently tackling this issue, and this book is not a scientific tome. But we don't totally get it yet. The same goes for sweeping. But the few things we do know about sweeping all start with the ice.

Curling ice is not like hockey ice. Yes, the game began on frozen ponds and lakes, but these days, curling ice is highly manicured. There are many around the world who specialize in this craft. We call them icemakers. Look, no one said we were super creative. Curling ice starts out like hockey ice, just frozen water laid down on sand or concrete, with a lot of care taken to ensure that the ice freezes at an even level. For obvious reasons, any tilt in the ice would greatly affect how curling stones travel, and we can't have that.

Once the ice freezes, it is treated with a refined water product that we call *pebble*. And why do we call it that? Because when it freezes on top of the ice, if you look at the ice from a worm's-eye view, it will appear as a bunch of small pebbles frozen on the surface. I know, I know. The creative thing. Here's how it looks:

The pebble helps the rocks curl, and also travel much faster than they would on natural ice. Looking back to the old frozen loch days in Scotland, I'd imagine that those Highlanders playing the earliest forms of curling would've had to shove those rocks pretty hard to get them to the other end. If you're a particularly perceptive person, you may have already discerned, then, what sweeping does. If you haven't, that's okay. I'm here for you.

Sweeping is a vigorous activity. It was once done with corn or straw brooms that looked like something your mom would use to sweep the front steps, or a witch would ride in a time of need. Now the brooms resemble something closer to a Swiffer, with a carbon-fibre handle and a head resting at the bottom that consists of a densely packed foam covered in fabric. That fabric caused a lot of consternation for a few seasons. They called it Broomgate. I think a guy made a podcast about it once. We'll talk about that a bit later.

With the energy generated by the sweeping, the pebble actually melts slightly as the rock travels over it. That slight melt reduces the friction between the rock and the ice, which allows the rock to travel farther and to stay a little bit straighter. It's part of how we know that pebble makes rocks curl. If you throw a regulation curling stone on hockey-arena ice or on a frozen pond, it will stay almost dead straight, regardless of how much you try to make it curl. But on pebbled ice, curl it does.

Making the rock go farther makes sense, but I've had people ask me before, "Well, why would you want a rock to stay straighter? Isn't the name of the game *curling*?" It is, but there is still an element of human error. There is still the physical act of throwing the stones. You may not throw the rock in exactly the way you want to. Or the skip, whose job it is to "read" the ice and tell you where to aim your throw, may get that calculation wrong. Sweeping can help minimize a small mistake.

Sweeping has also changed a lot over time, and we continue to learn much about it. There are university professors who study the physics of it. A curler named

Eugene Hritzuk, who lost a Canadian championship final and won a World Senior championship, has devoted his retirement to learning more about sweeping and the effects of different brush heads, sweeping patterns, ice conditions, and anything else that might affect the path of a rock. We've also learned in the last decade or so that, counterintuitively, sweeping might actually *help* make a rock curl.

For centuries, we really thought sweeping could only affect a rock's curl negatively (as in, a rock would curl less if we swept) and affect its speed. But we have figured out over the last decade that sweeping in a certain way, *with* the curl, might actually help the rock curl *more* than it used to. It has changed the way we play the game and has changed how we think about the game, too. It's no longer enough just to be a great shooter; you must also be a great sweeper to curl at the top levels of the sport. With this knowledge, we also have to accept that there may still be a lot we don't know about sweeping. If something we figured out just 10 years ago could change the game this much, maybe there's more on the horizon.

So there you have it. It's simple, really: sweeping helps the thrower make the shot. Yes, it does something. No, it's not just for show, or for something to do. And depending on who you ask, yes, the yelling helps. Much like a coxswain in rowing, a skip acts as a beacon of hope, someone to keep the sweepers on track, to help them help their teammate make the best shot. And yes, it is really, *really* hard. Seriously, go try it. I'll wait. Grab a mop or a brush in your house, put all your weight on it for 30 seconds while moving it back and forth as fast as you can, and then take a 60-second break. Then do it again. And then do it 58 more times. Oh, and you have to walk about seven kilometres total during those 60-second breaks. Don't worry, you can do it! At least, that's what any casual curling watcher will tell a curler.

Sweeping is just different now. This newfound need for strength and expert sweeping technique is why this isn't your grandfather's curling anymore. Curlers look more like athletes than they ever used to. They're big, they're tall, they're strong, and they're working out and pushing the pace as hard as any athlete in any other Olympic sport. And it's why you aren't any likelier to make the Olympics in curling than you are in downhill skiing or bobsled or ice hockey. Sorry, Gord.

CHAPTER 4

NO, YOU WILL NOT MAKE THE OLYMPICS IN CURLING

For years, curlers were haunted by a six-word phrase. You'd hear it uttered on television. Maybe at a comedy club as part of a comedian's set. You might hear it from your friends. Hell, I even heard it from my parents. *Curling is not a real sport.* Those people were inspired by seeing curlers on TV who maybe didn't look like traditional athletes. Some had beer bellies. A lot looked like car mechanics or convenience store owners or tradesmen.[1] You used to be allowed to smoke cigarettes while playing, a practice that wasn't banned until 1980. In some ways, you could understand the criticism. If you didn't play the game and had no familiarity with both its physicality and its nuance, it was easy to take those images and make broad assumptions.

---

1 Probably because they were. Curlers, Canadian ones especially, have a long tradition of holding down full-time jobs while maintaining the schedule and regimen of a professional athlete.

1
3
257

The Canadian Curling Association (now Curling Canada) felt those assumptions were so strong among the general public that in its push to make curling an Olympic sport, it forced some of Canada's top curlers to get on an exercise regimen, telling them they would be unable to represent Canada at the World Championships or at Olympic demonstrations if they didn't meet certain fitness criteria. This led to a famous public war between Curling Canada's head, Warren Hansen, and one of Canada's top curlers, Ed Werenich. In a world before social media, curling was fighting for legitimacy and listening to what it thought was the voice of the general public, crying out against the idea of curling as a sport and opposing its candidacy for the Olympics.

As so often happens with general outcry, those voices went unheard, and curling became a full-medal sport at the 1998 Winter Olympics in Nagano. At that time, no one would've accused a lot of the curlers of being in peak physical condition, but they were top athletes in their sport and deserved the opportunity to compete. As more nations became involved once Olympic glory was on the line, and as curling continued its march toward professionalism, curlers did begin to morph into athletes. There was no longer a lot for the general public to complain about with regards to curling being a sport. It became one of the more popular sports at the Olympics. Curlers got younger, fitter, faster. And so, instead of using the old six-word phrase, the general public adopted a new one: *I could make the Olympics in curling.*

In some ways, it's the same argument. If someone is not an Olympic-level athlete, then perhaps the way they could qualify for the Olympics without doing the work is by choosing the sport that seems the least like a sport. Well, I have some bad news for you. Unless you're 12 years old and you're already a reasonably good athlete, you won't be making the Olympics in curling. Especially if you live in Canada.

I know it's fun to imagine that being a good beer-league hockey player in your mid-30s would make you more than a good enough curler to get to the Olympics, but I just don't see that dream coming true for you. Here are a few reasons why you—yes, you—will not make the Olympics in curling:

1. I NEVER MADE THE OLYMPICS, AND I'VE CURLED WAY, WAY MORE THAN YOU HAVE.

In fact, I never even got close. In Canada, there is a tournament to get into the Olympics that we call the Roar of the Rings. Fun name. The format of both the tournament and how you qualify for it has changed a few times over the years, but, generally speaking, it's an eight-to-ten team tournament and you spend the three years before the Olympics curling and accruing World ranking points in order to qualify. If you don't have enough World ranking points, you may find yourself in what we call the Pre-Trials. Again, the format has changed a few times, but that's usually a tournament of 10 to 16 teams that qualifies one or two teams for the Roar of the Rings.

I curled for over 20 years, most of them at a highly competitive level, and I never made either of those tournaments. I threw tens of thousands of rocks. I toured all over the country playing in tournaments. I played against all the top teams. I won a handful of World Curling Tour events, I have seven BC provincial medals, and I never even made it into the tournament that gets you into the tournament that qualifies you for the Olympics.

The idea that you would start now, at whatever age you're at (again, if you are reading this and you are 12, you still have a chance—it's small, but it exists), and that you would just magically be good enough within four years to be in the Olympics is quite funny to think about. That's the other thing about this. People not only think they can make the Olympics in curling, but think it'll happen by the *next* Olympics. Sitting on their couch. Drinking a beer. Eating chips. Watching the elite athletes on their screen and thinking, "You know, if I really tried, I could be there by the time the next Olympics roll around."

When I was beginning my comedy career, I was asked to appear on a radio show and podcast hosted by the late and much-loved (including by me) Vancouver journalist Guy MacPherson. It was called *What's So Funny?* and it was one of the first podcasts about comedy ever. Guy had a ton of comedy luminaries on his show over the years, including Norm Macdonald, Colin Mochrie, Tom Green, Nikki Glaser, Marc Maron—the list goes on. It was an honour to be invited on. I only bring this up because one of the very first things Guy said when the discussion turned to curling was that he felt that if he started curling, he would be good enough to compete on a national level within six weeks. He wasn't joking. He was basing this on a past as a good basketball player. Not one who played at any sort of high level, but one who had played the game his whole life and considered himself a decent athlete. Well....

2. THE JARED ALLEN CONUNDRUM

As you learned in the opening pages of this book, once Jared Allen was finished being a very, very good football player in the NFL, he turned his attention to curling. Like many, he figured it might offer him a quick berth in the Olympics. And he had better reason than most for his confidence. Jared Allen is a very, very good *professional* athlete.

That was seven years ago, and Jared Allen has yet to win any major curling tournaments. He has yet to represent the United States in any sort of world championship.

He has played in three US National Championships, and his teams have gone a combined 4–19 at those championships. And it isn't because he's playing on bad teams, at least not on paper. In each case, he has been on a team skipped by a former US national champion. Not only that, but he's trying hard. He told me he's invested quite a bit of money in his curling journey, not to mention frequently practising and playing in curling leagues and tournaments every year to try to get better.

And in seven years, he hasn't won anything. This section doesn't exist to embarrass Jared Allen—quite the opposite, in fact. He's actually done extremely well in just seven years' time. Most curlers would not be competing at national championships in such a short timeframe. He is clearly very dedicated, wants to succeed in the sport, and is doing his very best to accomplish those goals. You know who else probably wants him to accomplish those goals? USA Curling. I'm sure it would love the media boom that would come with Jared accompanying a team to a World Championships or an Olympics—and in the States, they have the means to do so, as they name the team that competes at the Worlds, and they appoint an alternate for every Olympics. But they've decided each time that the good press wouldn't be enough to offset the fact that Jared isn't good enough yet. At *curling*.

So you, the non-athlete, or maybe the guy who was the star of his small town's high-school baseball team but hasn't picked up a bat in a decade, probably aren't going to get up off the couch and just waltz into the Olympics. If a guy with this much athletic pedigree, not that far removed from his career peak in one of the toughest sports in the world, can't make it, well, neither can you.

This is also conveniently not mentioning the fact that the US is not exactly a curling superpower. Although they did win the 2018 Olympic gold medal in an upset, the country hasn't won a men's World title since 1978. If Jared was Canadian, his prospects would be even more dire. Now I'm hearing you say, "Well, Canada and the US aren't the only teams at the Winter Olympics. There are even smaller countries there. And I have dual citizenship!" Well, isn't that convenient.

3. YOUR PASSPORT CANNOT HELP YOU

Canada and the United States competed in the last Olympics for curling. So did Sweden, Switzerland, Italy, South Korea, Japan, Great Britain... the list goes on. Maybe you're a dual-national. You know Canada is a curling power. I've laid out why you might not make it in the US either. But what if you parachuted into the country your grandparent was born in? Strangely enough, your prospects might be even worse, even if the pool of curlers in those countries is much shallower.

When the Olympics became a full-medal sport in 1998, countries very quickly realized that outside Canada, there was no sure-thing winner. Yes, there were the usual suspects always hanging around the podium with Canada, but those nations often relied on a single team to get them to the promised land, and didn't have strong depth in the sport. Knowing they could form teams and potentially compete rather seriously, rather quickly, a lot of traditionally non-curling nations started to invest money in the sport. China, for example, converted a bunch of athletes from other sports, sending them to Canada to train with our top coaches. Bingyu Wang began curling in 2001 and by 2009 had won a women's World Championship. In 2010, she won a bronze medal at the Olympics, China's first medal in a winter team sport.

Here's the thing, though: unless you are already an existing, young athlete who lives in that country and has a chance to be converted to curling, or who started curling at a young age in that country for some reason, you will not have the opportunity to play for your nation. Most countries other than Canada support between one and three teams per gender. Almost every single one of their curlers either had success as a junior curler in that country or came from another sport first.

For example, take seven-time World champion Niklas Edin, from Sweden. Edin came onto the men's scene after a very successful junior career. He arrived with his junior team as they aged into a men's team, and they had success on the global stage, making the 2010 Olympics and winning their first World title in 2013. After a bronze medal at the Sochi Olympics in 2014, three of Edin's team members left the sport. So what did he do? He picked up the best junior skip at that time, Oskar Eriksson, to help form a new squad. When they needed a new second in 2017? They picked up Rasmus Wranå, who was the top junior skip in Sweden at the time. Even really great junior curlers from Sweden, who grew up curling there, were getting left behind as their skips continually joined the team that was already the best in the nation. By cannibalizing his potential competition, Niklas Edin has represented Sweden at 12 of the last 13 World Championships, and the last four Olympics. I regret to inform you that your Swedish passport may only be good for discounts at Ikea.

I think the biggest irony in all this is that there are actually Winter Olympics sports that lend themselves to athletes getting ahead in them very quickly. Erin Jackson was a former inline speed skater and roller derby player who was recruited to become a speed skater and, four months later, made her first Olympics. Many bobsledders in various countries and various Games are converted athletes from other sports, usually football or other disciplines that require being large and fast, like track-and-field events such as shot put and hammer throw.

But again, these are all people who are already athletes and then convert. Curling is a sport whose strategy demands years of study. Its physical precision requires years of practice, countless rocks thrown in small-town curling clubs. It simply isn't good enough to be strong or fast or dedicated. I'm sorry.

And I mean that in the most Canadian way possible.

CHAPTER 5

IT'S TIME TO PLAY THE GAME

Curling is a bit of a complicated sport, and I understand that. There are no basic rules for the casual fan to intuit. For example, in soccer, even if you know nothing about the intricacies of offside and what constitutes a yellow card versus a red card, you can understand that the goal is to put the ball into the net. By contrast, most people don't even know how curling is scored. They certainly don't know what the brooms do (fortunately, we covered that) or how much the rocks weigh (42 pounds) or a lot of the terminology. When I was working on my podcast *Broomgate*, showrunner Kathleen Goldhar came on the road with me to do the interviews that made up the bulk of the show, and she told me that when I was talking with other curlers off the record, she couldn't even follow the conversation, as though we were speaking a different language.

I want as many people as possible to be part of the curling conversation, so I'm going to attempt to unpack some of that language for you here. Sometimes books will use a glossary. This is like that, but instead of just listing a bunch of definitions, I figure the best way to describe the sport to you is to take you inside an end. So let's do that now. If you come across a word you don't know yet and it's *italicized*, you don't have to worry, because it's coming up soon on our action-glossary (except for *italicized*; I'm not defining that). Come and play an end of curling with me, and let's have some fun learning about the game together.

END: A division of play within a curling game. The best comparison is an inning in baseball. Most curling games will consist of either eight or ten ends. Scoring is done at the end of each end, once each team has thrown eight rocks. Only one team scores per end.

Welcome to Prince Albert, Saskatchewan, home of the 2025 Curling Rocks! Invitational. We have reached the final, and we are in for a doozy! It's Team Scotty Skip facing off against Team Horrible Evil Bad Guys for the grand prize: $500, a lovely set of Coleman camping lanterns, and two toasters, and the team will have to argue among themselves about who will take them home!

The teams begin the game by drawing to the *button* to see who will get the *hammer*. Whichever team gets closest will start the game with the advantage of the hammer, and will therefore throw last. And would you look at that, a perfectly swept rock right to the button for Scotty Skip and his team of Tommy Third, Sammy Second, and Johnny Lead. (You knew I was naming the lead Johnny. Whether this is related to me playing lead my entire career is irrelevant.)

HAMMER: The team who throws the final stone in the end is said to have the hammer. It's an advantage because your final shot will decide how the scoring plays out. If you score any number of points with the hammer, the hammer flips to the other team in the next end.

BUTTON: This is the circle directly in the centre of the *house*. In the middle of that is what we call the "pin."

As is curling custom, the teams now shake hands and begin the game. The Horrible Evil Bad Guys are up first, and their lead decides to throw up a centre *guard* with his first rock. Because of the *free guard zone*, Scotty Skip and his team won't be able to remove it from play.

GUARD: A rock thrown to end up within the field of play, but not in the *house*. As the name suggests, it is intended to guard future rocks that will end up in the house. Depending on ice conditions, generally speaking, an effective guard is one that ends up about halfway between the *hog line* and the *house*.

FREE GUARD ZONE: The free guard zone was introduced in the '90s to make curling games more exciting (save your barbs about them still not being exciting, please). At first, the rule stated that any rocks thrown as guards could not be removed from play until the fourth stone of the end, i.e., the second rock thrown by the team with the hammer. It has since been extended twice, and the sport now uses a five-rock FGZ, meaning that any rocks thrown as guards cannot be removed until the sixth stone of an end.

Johnny Lead, who has had an excellent tournament so far, and is also quite handsome, steps into the *hack* and readies to throw his first stone. Knowing that he cannot remove the guard from play, his team decides to have him throw a guard of his own, but he will throw it off of the centre line: a *corner guard*.

HACK: These are the blocks the curlers use to push themselves out toward the other end to deliver the stone. They resemble starting blocks for a runner. There are two blocks, one on each side of the centre line. Right-handed throwers will throw from the left hack, and left-handed throwers will throw from the right.

CORNER GUARD: A guard that is delivered away from the centre line, usually about two to four feet from it. It is designed to encourage offence for a team with the hammer.

With Johnny Lead making a beautiful and perfect corner guard, the Very Evil lead on the other team decides to throw a *draw* around the centre guard they played a stone before. This is the first time the play will be brought into the *house*. Unfortunately for Team Evil, it is a little bit heavy, and while it stays in the rings, it is behind the tee line.

DRAW: A shot designed to come to rest in the house without removing an opponent's stone.

HOUSE: The four concentric rings that make up the scoring target in curling. It looks like a bullseye. The house is 12 feet in diameter, and since we aren't very good at naming stuff in curling, all the rings are named after their diameter, except for the button (see above). The rings are the 12-foot, 8-foot, 4-foot, and button. Rocks cannot score unless they are touching the house.

TEE LINE: This is a line that bisects the curling house laterally. Because there is also a centre line which, as you might imagine, runs vertically down the exact middle of the sheet, this line that bisects the curling house also runs through the centre line, creating a T shape directly in the centre of the house. Again, not very original at naming stuff. It's also the name of Marc Bulger's curling bar in Nashville (see Chapter 1).

With that draw coming a little bit deep into the house, Scotty Skip will now ask Johnny Lead to throw a *freeze*. It's a shot that requires quite a bit of precision, but it's no trouble for Johnny Lead, and he makes it perfectly, making sure to let the rock go before the *hog line* in the process.

FREEZE: A shot that is like a draw but is intended to come to rest right in front of an opposition's stone in the house. Most of the time, a perfect freeze is one that is directly in front of an opponent's stone and just touching it, with no separation between the two.

HOG LINE: There are two hog lines on the ice, one at each end, drawn 21 feet from the tee line. At the throwing end, a thrower *must* release the stone before any part of the stone touches the hog line. If they let it go after that, an official may remove the stone from play. At the far end, or the scoring end, the hog line delineates the field of play. A stone must fully cross the hog line at the scoring end to be considered in the field of play. If it ends up short, it is called a "hogged" rock, and it is removed from play. Curling tradition also dictates that the curler who hogged the stone owes their team a beer after the game for the screw-up.

The lead rocks have now concluded. Each team consists of four positions (see Chapter 3) and each position throws two rocks. It's now the seconds' turn to throw. Given how good Johnny Lead made the freeze, the dastardly second for the Evils has been asked to throw another freeze on top of Johnny Lead's stone. And even evil wins sometimes, as the second makes it perfectly, and they sit *shot*.

SHOT STONE: This is the stone that is counting at any given point in an end. Refer to Chapter 3 for how curling is scored, but stones can be multiples of shot as well. For example, shot stone is the rock closest to the button. Second shot is the rock that is second-closest. Third shot is third-closest, etc. Knowing which stone is shot at a given time is crucial for developing strategy throughout an end.

With three rocks now behind the centre guard and the Evils sitting shot, the brilliant boys led by Scotty Skip have decided the centre guard is a problem, and given that we are now outside the scope of the free guard zone, with Sammy Second's first shot, Scotty Skip decides to *peel*. Sammy Second makes the peel without much difficulty.

PEEL: A shot designed to remove a stone from play, while ensuring that the stone being thrown also leaves play. It is often used to clear a guard from the front of the house.

After Sammy Second executes the peel, it makes sense for the Evils to put the guard back up. But uh-oh... the stone being thrown by their second slides into the top of the house! Given that it is so close to the three rocks that are frozen behind it, Scotty Skip calls for the *runback takeout.*

TAKEOUT: A rock thrown at a speed designed to remove one or more of the opponent's stones from play. It differs from a peel in that it is usually thrown with the goal of keeping your thrown stone in play afterwards.

RUNBACK: A type of takeout where a player will "run" another stone "back" into an opposition stone. This is usually called for if there is a distance between two stones greater than four feet, and the term is usually used to describe running a guard back onto a stone in the house. Either you're running the stone back in order to sit shot (i.e., you're running your red guard onto a yellow stone in the house) or, as in this case, you're running the stone back toward a pile of rocks to try and remove as many as you can from play.

Sammy Second is a pretty good player, so he makes the runback! He gets rid of two of the three stones that are on the button, leaving the stone he just threw as a guard just outside the house, while the one he ran back hits the pile of stones and rolls away from those stones into the open, meaning it is no longer behind any guards.

It's now onto third stones, and the Evils are lying shot stone, but Team Scotty Skip has a rock that is also counting second shot (remember about shot stones from before?). The Evils decide with their no-good, terrible third's first shot that they will throw a *hit and roll* on the second shot stone belonging to Team Scotty Skip, and try to roll another stone behind the guard.

HIT AND ROLL: It's a takeout, but where the plan is to hit the opposition's rock in such a way that your thrown stone rolls to a desired location. This is usually behind a guard or in front of an opposition stone.

The third lets it go, and it's a little wide! The Evil skip calls for the sweep, but it's not the usual "*Hurry hard!*" or "*Yes!*" that you're used to hearing. He's using a different word: "*Carve! Carve it!*"

CARVE: The act of having one sweeper sweep a stone *with* the curl, and not against it. The prevailing theory in curling is that by doing so, you actually help the stone to curl a little bit more.

Unfortunately, the carving is not enough, and the rock doesn't make contact with the opposition stone at all. It's a no-good, terrible shot from the Evils' no-good, terrible third. He has completely *flashed* it.

FLASH: When you're throwing a takeout and you completely fail to make contact with the intended target. Because you threw takeout weight (*weight* is the term we use to describe the speed at which you've thrown the stone), it also means the shot you threw goes right through the house and out of play.

This leaves Team Scotty Skip with a choice. They have their rock just outside the house, in front of the Evils' shot stone. They could run it back again. But if they do that, they risk hitting out their own stone, which is sitting a few feet away from the Evils' shot stone. So they decide it might be less risky to play the *chase*. It will require some precision, but Tommy Third is up to the task, and he makes it perfectly. Team Scotty Skip is now lying two! (*Lying* is the word we use as a stand-in for who has shot stone at any given time. For example, there could be six stones in the house at any given time, but if you are lying two, that means you have the shot stone and the second shot stone.)

CHASE: When a rock is either partly or fully covered by a guard, a team may elect to play a takeout with a slightly softer weight than a usual takeout. As you might imagine, if the rock is going slower, it will curl more, making it more likely to remove the stone behind the guard.

With the chase made, the Evils are now facing two counters (stones that will count as points) for Team Scotty Skip. Luckily for them, Tommy Third's chase stone rolled toward the other one already in the house, just in front of it, and so they call the *tap* to try and create a wall of stones, making their own rock harder to remove. The Evils' third is less terrible this time, and he makes it, leaving the bad guys lying one.

TAP: A draw shot thrown with a bit of extra weight, designed to move a stone in the house but not remove it from play. This is usually done to set up a barrier of stones behind your own stone, making it harder to remove.

With the Evils lying one, there isn't a great way to remove the stone without touching their back ones, but Tommy Third is pretty good, so Scotty asks him to throw a tough shot: a *pick*. Tommy makes it but unfortunately removes one of their two back stones, so Team Scotty Skip is only lying one.

PICK: This is like a peel, but is done on a rock inside the house. The task is to hit just a small piece of the designated stone to "pick" it out of the rings and to avoid hitting other stones behind it.

We're now at skip stones, and the Evils call the obvious, another hit and roll to try and get back behind that centre guard. Unfortunately, the rock rolls a little too far, and it ends up between the centre guard and the corner guard (remember all the way back at the start of the end, when Team Scotty Skip threw that corner guard?). So now the call is easy for Scotty: he wants to hit and roll behind the corner guard himself. And he makes it! Team Scotty Skip is lying one, completely covered by the guard.

It's the Evils' last shot, and they figure their only chance of achieving their goal of getting the hammer back while only giving up one point is to draw around the centre guard, hoping that Scotty will miss a chase or a runback opportunity. Unfortunately for them, it ends up a little too heavy and slides through the rings.

Now Scotty could just draw to anywhere in the rings for two, but he doesn't feel that confident about where to put the broom down for a target, as he just saw the Evils' skip miss his shot. So he decides to play the *raise*, tapping his own team's guard in for two.

He makes it, and the crowd goes absolutely wild!

RAISE: Typically a draw shot (you can also refer to a runback as a "raise takeout," but that has fallen out of favour in recent years), this is a shot designed to promote or "raise" a stone from a defensive position to an offensive one. So it could mean tapping a guard into the house to score, as in this scenario, or it could mean raising a stone from a spot already in the house, maybe near the top, to somewhere farther back in the house.

If you're wondering, Team Scotty Skip ends up winning the game 8–1. They *forced* the Evils to 1 in the second, and then after *blanking* the third and fourth ends, they scored three more in the fifth, and *stole* one in the sixth, seventh, and eighth ends to win. They have defeated evil once again and are looking forward to their annual camping trip, now that they have four beautiful lanterns.

FORCE: When you do not have the hammer, your goal is to get it back. The cheapest way to get the hammer back is when your opposition scores only one point. We call this a *force*, because you have *forced* your opposition to give the hammer back to you with the minimum amount of damage.

BLANK: If no points are scored in an end, then the team that had the hammer in the previous end retains it. Since teams are looking to score multiple points with the hammer, you will see a team with the hammer potentially clear an opposition stone from the rings with their final shot, to keep the hammer to the next end.

STEAL: If you score any number of points in an end where you don't have the hammer, that is referred to as a *steal*. Because the team with the hammer is expected to score, you have stolen the points from them.

Congratulations, you are now ready for the curling club lounge. First beer's on you.

S.S. NOVA SCOTIA

CHAPTER 6

MY FAVOURITE END EVER #1

Ferbey versus Dacey, 2004 Brier Final, 10th End

Curling is a game made up of ends. It started with 14 (turns out there was nothing else to do in the 1950s?), then moved to 12, then 10. And now, most of the time, we play eight. For a sport that has such clear divisions in how the time of the game is spent, it's interesting how few ends really get remembered. Sure, games get remembered, and shots get remembered, but curling doesn't have a discussion of great ends in the way that baseball does of great innings. Maybe it's because of the hammer and its importance to an end's trajectory. So often, when we speak of curling, we speak of those great hammer shots—shots that impacted the score of an end or the score of a game so greatly that they get etched into the annals of the sport. Plus, they're easy. They're quick. Even the slowest shot only takes about 10 seconds to accurately depict on a highlight reel. We'll look at some of those moments later on in this book, when we discuss the game's best shots, some of the game's great players, and my own personal failures as a curler.

But what about *ends*? Most of the best ends take time. They let you sit with them, as when you're rereading a page of a brilliant book because you couldn't take in the splendour of the writing on your first attempt. Curling does have a time limit, with each team getting a set amount of time on the clock. How this time is meted out has changed every decade or so, but it can be most simply explained as each team being "on the clock" when it is their turn to throw. A team's clock is stopped when their opponents are strategizing or throwing. Curling currently uses what is commonly described as "thinking time," meaning that while a rock is travelling down the ice, the clocks for both teams are stopped. It only took roughly 25 years of timing games to figure out that draw shots take, at minimum, double the time to travel down the ice than hit shots do, and that it was probably unfair to count the time the rock travels on a team's individual time clock.

I would be remiss if I didn't mention the best part about the timing of curling, which is the punishment for running out of time. They closed America's most dangerous and most secure prison, Alcatraz, in 1963 (the fact that they called Alcatraz "the Rock" may or may not be part of its inclusion here), but in the spirit of that island tomb, curling's punishment for running out of time is without comparison, particularly in sports—if your team runs out of time, you simply cannot throw another rock. Your game is effectively over. So if you run out of time with four rocks left, your opponent could finish the game with four shots in a row. Four hammers, if you will. Even if the game isn't particularly close, running out of time almost always ends in an automatic loss. Even being disallowed to throw a single stone could have an immeasurable impact on the game. I mean, imagine Thor with four hammers. Imagine a hockey team only being allowed to possess the puck for a certain amount of time per game, and if they pass that amount of time, the whole team has to leave the ice and let the other team impose its will on their goaltender. You can't. But curling can.

So what does all this timing stuff have to do with what we're talking about? Well, because teams are individually timed and that time is based on how long it takes to make a shot call/throw a shot, some ends happen very quickly. A team that communicates well and is throwing eight hit shots can get through an end in less than a minute on the time clock. Which means that if a game goes by with relative speed and ease, teams can have many minutes left with which to play a final end. If the first end of a game takes two minutes combined, a final end could take 30. This might sound bad to you. You might be one of those people who refuses to watch basketball because the final minute of a basketball game takes 20 minutes to play, with all the timeouts. Well, the difference, in curling, is that you have access to everything these teams are thinking and saying to each other. Everyone is on microphone, and the world's best curlers are telling you exactly what they're about to do and why they're about to do it. Something tells me you might find the last minute of the NBA Finals more engaging if you knew everything LeBron was saying during every time-out. It's one of the things that makes curling extremely good: that the best part of the game takes the longest. You'd love to see that in other sports. The ninth inning of baseball now has six outs. The third period in hockey is now 30 minutes. Golf is now only three holes (it's unfortunate that the only way to make golf more exciting is to play less of it, but it's my book and I make the rules).

And so it is that one of my favourite ends happened in 2004, before the advent of thinking time. Back then, they just gave teams the ungodly sum of 73 minutes apiece with which to play the game, including rock-travelling time. It was a mess. (How did we arrive at 73 minutes? Why did we think "Hey, let's force the curlers to play faster" and then give them a combined time of *one hundred and forty-six minutes*? We've gotten better at this.) And it was before curlers wore clothes that fit them properly. It was the Brier final (Canada's men's national championship), and Alberta was playing Nova Scotia. Alberta was represented by Randy Ferbey, a powerhouse of a curler, a first-ballot hall of famer if such a thing existed in the sport, who won Brier titles in two decades and whose team was known as the "Ferbey Four," one of curling's first teams to brand itself and transcend the usual boundaries of the sport. Nova Scotia was represented by Mark Dacey, who made it to the Brier six times and had lost the final the year before. For his part, Dacey was unbranded and at no point tried to sell curling mittens with his face on them. A missed opportunity, to be sure.

It was a David-versus-Goliath matchup. Dacey had lost the Brier final the year before to this very same Ferbey rink. (Yes, curling teams are referred to collectively as "rinks," and so yes, that does mean the rinks play on the rink. Like I said, we are bad at naming things.) But he had only played one Grand Slam event ever, and his team was cursed by living in an Atlantic province, where competition was hard to come by. Further, to this point, Nova Scotia as a province had won the Brier only twice, with the last win coming 53 years before, in 1951. Randy Ferbey's rink themselves had won more Brier titles in the previous three years than Nova Scotia had won in its history. The Ferbey Four were looking to sell just a few more pairs of branded mittens that spring by winning their fourth straight Brier title and creating the brand synergy dreams are made of. And they looked well on their way, leading 8–4 heading into the eighth end, which, at this point in the sport's history, was pretty much a done deal.

At this point, teams did not come back from that deficit, and they certainly didn't do it against Ferbey.

But Dacey had managed to cobble something together that looked like a potential comeback. In that eighth end, after David Nedohin, Randy Ferbey's fourth thrower,[1] missed a relatively easy double takeout to make the end essentially moot, Dacey had two rocks clearly in the house and a third just nibbling the back of the rings. After a measurement determined that the rock was on, Dacey scored 3 and the world started to wonder if Ferbey was slipping in an era when he never slipped. Dacey forced Ferbey to 1 in the ninth, and set the stage for my absolute favourite curling end of all time, an end that had it all: big makes, huge misses, fights with the crowd, momentum swings, mustaches, and ugly brooms.

It all starts with Marcel Rocque of the Alberta rink—a mountain of a man, a guy who'd tell you he was an elite curler and you weren't sure if he said *curler* or *football player*. He revolutionized sweeping in the sport, in the sense that he and Scott Pfeifer (or "Huffin and Puffin," as they were known colloquially) were both very good at it; they had the type of sweeping ability that even the most untrained curling eye could tell was *good*. You could feel Rocque's power when he swept. It helped that

1 If the person who throws last is someone other than the skip, they are referred to as the "fourth."

he was perpetually sweaty, would keep the top of his three-button collar undone so you could see part of his barrel chest, and had managed to retain just the slightest of French accents despite growing up in Alberta. He had the vibe of someone you'd meet at the docks, under the only working street lamp, as boxes of questionable origin were changing hands in his midst. If you only watched him on television and didn't know him, he seemed scary in a way that very few curlers did. Curlers aren't an overly intimidating bunch. But Marcel had the juice, and he was a joy to watch.

The 10th end opened with two rocks from Rocque, and it started the way Ferbey started most of his ends when they were in the lead without the hammer: by drawing his first two rocks into the house. This was a style that was first used by Ferbey and copied by many after. Before this, not wanting to throw guards, teams would often throw one rock in the house and the other through the rings, or even both through the rings, trusting their ability to make enough hits to secure the win. The rationale behind this was that you beat your opponent—who needs to score—to the centre of the house, and by doing it twice and giving them two stones to remove, scoring becomes even harder. Unfortunately for Rocque, this time he makes the tiniest of mistakes and his two rocks overlap just slightly. One aphorism we love to use in curling and that you hear in other sports is that "it's just a game of inches," and while you might also hear that same sentence used in some divorce proceedings, it holds true for our game perhaps more than most. Even if, technically, we should be using metric.

The next few shots are almost nothing to speak of. With Ferbey hoping to keep the house clear to ensure Dacey doesn't get two points, and Dacey wanting to keep the house a little messier to ensure that he does, the two teams trade off by throwing guards (Dacey) and removing them (Ferbey). Then the end starts to heat up.

Curling, at its absolute apex, is a test of wills. People often describe tennis in this way, but tennis has the benefit of being a very *fast-moving* test of wills. Yes, it is a game of momentum, and yes, you need nerves of steel, but you're always moving, trusting your muscle memory to carry you through even the most difficult and nervous of times. Curling is like that, except you get between 30 and 300 seconds before your shot to decide to park those nerves and make it. Curling is a test of wills, except the stones are stationary and your opponent cannot do a single thing to affect your shot, other than by putting their rocks in difficult positions to deal with. The "test of wills" in curling is the very concept of wills, as though wills are some out-of-body third person, screaming at you, saying things like "*Haha, I bet you're gonna miss this!*" and "Remember when you had this same shot on this same sheet four days ago... *and you missed it? Hahahaha loser!*"

You're facing your opponent, but you're also battling your own mind in a way that other sports just do not make room for. Remember, the prescribed length of game here, not counting timeouts and the fifth-end break, is *one hundred and forty-six minutes*. It's a long time to be with your thoughts while trying to execute a sporting task. And the battle of wills here starts on the 10th shot of the end, when Nova Scotia third Bruce Lohnes steps into the hack to throw his first rock.

If Marcel Rocque looks like a football player, Bruce Lohnes looks like a curler. If you had never met your office's tech guy, and Bruce walked by you at your office, you'd think, "I bet he's probably the tech guy." He even wore glasses with a slight tint to them on the ice, as if to suggest that the showy glare of curling was too much for his eyes. With one guard remaining above the house and the two Rocque rocks (I know, I know) staggered still, skip Dacey calls for a draw around the two rocks. This type of shot, a draw around a rock that's already in the house, is only possible on championship ice, manicured to perfection with a maximum amount of curl.

If this end were being played in a curling club on a smoky Sunday evening, this chapter would be five sentences long and Ferbey would've won the game 8–6. Despite the game being played on the best ice available to the players, the difficulty of this shot is still extremely high, and you can immediately sense the panic in Lohnes's voice. The wills have come alive, and Bruce is losing the battle. He does not want to play the shot. You can see it in his face and hear it in his voice. He doesn't actually have an issue with the called shot—the team doesn't really have a choice. It's the only play to try to secure the needed two points, with the bonus that if things break right, it could lead to three. His issue is with the way Dacey wants him to throw it. Dacey wants him to throw the out-turn—meaning that he would aim for the rock to travel down the outside of the sheet to get around the two rocks, plus the guard in front. The outsides of a curling sheet get played less often, and therefore can be a bit tricky to read. Lohnes, naturally, wants the easier option, which is to come down the middle, with the in-turn. Dacey isn't interested, even with lead Andrew Gibson also objecting. You can actually hear the players' mics pick up Gibson saying "Oh my god" under his breath when Dacey won't capitulate. He knows, as does Lohnes—as, no doubt, does Dacey himself—that a miss here probably seals the game for Ferbey. Luckily for Nova Scotia, Lohnes half-makes it. He comes to the back of the house, wide open, and Ferbey elects to hit the guard, which, despite his four World titles and very successful career, he probably still thinks about.

Did Ferbey have a ton of options? He could've hit the open one instead of the guard, or gotten very daring and frozen to it. But he was up by two points, and peeling the guard, in his view, would've ensured they would never give up more than a deuce. He forgot one thing: in addition to wearing tinted glasses, Bruce Lohnes is, in this moment, one of the best curlers on the entire planet, and in this particular Brier final, he has saved his best shot for last. If the wills overtook him on his first shot, on his second shot, he enters some sort of fugue state. Even taking a timeout and elongating the amount of time the wills can burrow into the back of his head, they can't shake him, as he realizes that the only option is to repeat the shot he just threw, but with more precision. When we think of the biggest shots in curling, we often think of the spectacular makes to win games, many of which are featured elsewhere in this book. Skips are paid the big bucks to make the big shots, they say. This often leaves thirds in the lurch. But make no mistake, this shot is as big or as important as any in the Brier's history. Lohnes makes the shot perfectly, buried behind cover and impossible to remove. He has all but ensured that unless some massive mistake by Mark Dacey occurs, they will at the very least score two and make it to an extra end.

Randy Ferbey still needs his fourth thrower, Dave Nedohin, to make a couple of shots to ensure that extra end happens. He elects to hit the open one, Lohnes's first, and the wills continue to take over the end, because something happens that we will sometimes see elite athletes do when they feel like something is slipping out of their grasp: they look to blame someone else. After Dave Nedohin's first shot (which he makes), he immediately swings around to glare at someone in the crowd. Marcel Rocque twigs to this as well, and if we weren't scared of him before, we are now, as he points at the figure in the crowd—who has apparently been needling Nedohin in the hack before he shoots, a huge no-no—and tells him that after the game, it'll be "you and me. One more word, you and me." Then he balls his fist up, stretching the limit of what a curling glove can hold, ready to take out his frustration on his early rock set-up, Lohnes's excellent shot, and the feeling that a fourth consecutive Brier title is floating away on a Bluenose. The Brier typically does some of the best ratings of any sporting event on The Sports Network—Canada's answer to ESPN—but I can only imagine what the ratings would've been for Fight Night: Rocque vs. Man in Stands if it had aired directly after the game.

It's rare that the final three shots of a 10th end in a Brier final that is decided by one point aren't that exciting, but they really pale in comparison with what has come before us in one of the most dramatic comebacks in the sport's history. Nedohin hits the open Nova Scotia stone and rolls out of the house, leaving just three rocks in play: the two Rocque draws that opened the end, and Lohnes's improbable shootout-at-the-OK-Corral moment, perfectly buried behind them. The team calls their second and final timeout to discuss what Mark Dacey should do with his first stone, and the early consensus seems to be that he needs to also bury a rock behind the two Rocque stones that are looking increasingly lonely at the top of the rings. However, this game isn't done with giving us excellent moments. While it's true that the final three shots aren't as exciting as the few that came just before, the second Nova Scotia timeout leads to one of the great moments in Brier history.

That moment? When Rob Harris, the Nova Scotia second, says one of the most absurd things anyone has ever said in the midst of a high-pressure situation like this: "I think if Mark makes the shot, we win the Brier." No one in the history of sports psychology would ever recommend saying this to someone who is about to attempt the second-biggest shot of their life, followed by their biggest, but fortunately this was 2004 and sports psychologists were blissfully unaware of curling teams, their phones remaining silent and unbothered by combatants in the roaring game.[2] And so it was that in 2004, Rob

---

2 Compare this with today, when two of the top five men's teams in Canada don't even have a traditional curling coach, but are "coached" at national events by sports psychologists. Kevin Koe, Olympian and three-time Brier champion, is coached by John Dunn, and Matt Dunstone, two-time Canadian junior champion and 2020 Brier bronze medallist, is coached by Adam Kingsbury, himself an Olympic coach with Rachel Homan in 2018.

Harris, in the biggest game of his life, repeated two more times that all Mark Dacey had to do was attempt this very difficult shot again, and if he made it, his team would achieve their lifelong dream of winning the national championship. Of course, the nagging subtext here is that if he missed it, they might lose said Brier. The funniest part of this, to me, is that he actually says the words "If we make this, we win the Brier." He even names the championship. He could've said something simpler, like "If we make this, we win the game," or something even softer, like "If we make this, we're in good shape." But no, he said "the Brier," and it is one of my favourite quotes in sports history, as though Roberto Alomar told Joe Carter before he went to bat in the 1993 World Series' Game 6 that he should probably hit a home run because that would mean they'd win the World Series.

Bruce Lohnes, who has now finished his shooting and has re-emerged on Earth, looks at Harris and says, "We don't need to win the Brier right now," which is funny because, of course, technically they can't, since Alberta still has a stone remaining. They decide to draw using the original in-turn path Lohnes wanted to use, and Dacey makes it fine enough, but leaves a path for Nedohin to follow him down with a freeze and potentially force Dacey into a very difficult shot to score two—and force an extra end. But Nedohin misses, Dacey is left with the improbable draw for 3, and he makes it and gives Nova Scotia their first Brier title in five decades.

Mark Dacey is a curler who gets forgotten about quite a bit, but he's appeared at five Briers, medalled in four of them, and won one of them. It's an impressive record for a team from Nova Scotia especially, a province that is typically very difficult to succeed out of at the national level. Not only has the province not won a Brier since Dacey in 2004, but it has appeared in only one final since, and that was the year after, when Shawn Adams lost the final of the 2005 Brier to this same Ferbey team, who finally claimed their fourth title. As for the rest of 2004? Dacey would go on to a bronze-medal finish at the Worlds in Gävle, Sweden, and would return to the Brier just once more, winning a bronze there in 2006. But he'll forever be in my memory for what is one of the best and most entertaining ends of the game ever played, a story in sporting drama that took place over 25 unforgettable minutes in March 2004, when the Ferbey Four were finally beatable, Bruce Lohnes made one of the greatest shots in history, and Marcel Rocque almost punched a guy. Win the Brier, indeed.

CHAPTER 7

A CAUSE FOR CELEBRATION

Curling's Greatest-Ever Cellies

For hundreds of years, curling has been a sport concerned mostly with decorum. That does seem hard to believe, given the fact that the game involves a dramatic amount of screaming compared with most other sports, but it's true. Often called "the Gentleman's Game" (antiquated term, but I digress), curling starts and ends each game with handshakes between the two opposing teams. You aren't meant to do anything to embarrass or upstage the other team, and for a long time, part of the game's unwritten code even included the winning team buying the losers a beer. That's not even in cash leagues or big tournaments. If you won your Tuesday night rec league game, you actually lost money on that proposition. Curling was one of the few sports where it actually paid to lose.

On top of that, curling's officialdom gets in on the action, with rule books printed with opening pages on

"The Spirit of Curling," indicating that rules are meant to be followed, but that if everyone also just agreed to be a nice person and get along with everyone else, the rule book wouldn't even matter. This passage is directly from World Curling's rule book and website:

> Curling is a game of skill and of tradition. A shot well executed is a delight to see and it is also a fine thing to observe the time-honoured traditions of curling being applied in the true spirit of the game. Curlers play to win, but never to humble their opponents. A true curler never attempts to distract opponents, nor to prevent them from playing their best, and would prefer to lose rather than to win unfairly.
>
> Curlers never knowingly break a rule of the game, nor disrespect any of its traditions. Should they become aware that this has been done inadvertently, they will be the first to divulge the breach.
>
> While the main object of the game of curling is to determine the relative skill of the players, The Spirit of Curling demands good sportsmanship, kindly feeling and honourable conduct.
>
> This spirit should influence both the interpretation and the application of the rules of the game and also the conduct of all participants on and off

the ice.[1] Over years and years, curling adhered to this decorum, and that even extended to moments of great joy. Some of the biggest victories in the history of curling have been met with a whimper and a sigh, with teams focusing more on making sure they shake their opponents' hands than on celebrating with each other. The only other sport that comes close to this is hockey, where teams are expected, after a long and hard-fought playoff series, to enter into a handshake line where they pay respect to the other team. Must be a Canadian thing. The big difference, however, between curling and hockey is that in hockey, the losing team is made to wait while the other team celebrates like crazy, throwing equipment into the air, barrelling over the goaltender, and hugging each other individually before entering the handshake line. Most other sports don't end with any sort of parlay between the winning and losing teams: the loser is simply banished to their locker room while the other team cheers until their throats get sore.

Over the years, however, there has been the slightest of disruptions in decorum. As curling has increasingly

1 "Spirit of Curling," World Curling, https://worldcurling.org/curlclean/principles-and-values/.

professionalized and curlers have dedicated more and more time to their craft, the wins have started to feel like they mean a little bit more. Don't get me wrong, I'm sure every team that's won a big curling title has been excited. But over the last few decades, we have seen curlers start to celebrate in a manner more befitting their massive accomplishments, and I'll just say it: the sport is better for it. Without further ado, here are the five best celebrations in curling history, in no order. Well, and some honourable mentions too. I love celebrations! Let's get wild!

BRAD JACOBS

"COME ON!!"

2013 Roar of the Rings versus Kevin Martin

Brad Jacobs and his team of Ryan Fry and brothers E.J. and Ryan Harnden were beginning to gain attention in the 2014 Olympic quadrennial, as they won the Brier earlier in 2013 and were heading toward qualifying to be Canada's team at the Sochi Olympics. They were also gaining attention from tailors, as their custom became having the sleeves and torsos of their uniforms taken in to show off their bulging biceps.[2] Other curling teams

2 The curling world coined the term *schmeedium* in the wake of this pattern. It is, of course, a portmanteau of the words *small* and *medium*, and refers to the practice of having the shirt be different sizes in different areas in order to look its most ridiculous.

and curling athletes had made physical fitness a big part of their preparation and training regime, but no one had taken it to the extent that Team Jacobs had, and people were beginning to notice just how much the entire team looked like athletes.

It wasn't enough to *look* like an athlete though; they also wanted to *act* like athletes from other sports, and that came to the forefront at the 2013 Roar of the Rings. It was the second-to-last game of the round robin, and with both teams undefeated, the winner of this game would get an automatic bye to the final. Kevin Martin won the 2010 Olympic gold medal, and had made it clear that this year would be his swan song as a player. He was the incumbent and had the added mojo of wanting to retire on top. But young Jacobs was having none of that.

After making one of the nicest shots in curling history, a raise double-tap for two, Jacobs and company lost their minds. Jacobs screamed "*Yeah!*" at the top of his lungs. Ryan Fry, the third, did a peacock strut in front of the house, careful not to trip over any of the rocks while shouting encouragement at the skipper. Second E.J. Harnden went in for a high five that would rip the arm off a normal man.

Being sure to take time to shake the hands of his downed opponents, Jacobs finished by turning to the crowd at Winnipeg's MTS Centre and said, "*Come on!*" raising his hands violently in the air. As if that weren't enough, he repeated the trick two more times, looking at all corners of the stadium as he did it. The stadium obliged, cheering on their gladiator, who looked as though he had just defeated several lions. While that may not have been the case, he had defeated one Old Bear. He would ride the momentum from that victory to a win in the final and a berth in the 2014 Olympics, which he won, keeping Canada's gold medal streak at the Olympics alive. Although some of the celebrations on this list happened before this one, it's safe to say that Jacobs set the table for the general acceptance of big celebrations in the sport. Like...

PAT SIMMONS

The Broom Ejector

2015 Brier final versus Brad Jacobs

It's fitting that this celebration came against the man himself, Brad Jacobs. Some celebrations are not only about the celebration itself, but about the story behind it. Coming into the Brier, Team Morris was actually skipped by John Morris, who had joined after Kevin Koe departed following the 2014 Brier to join a new team for the 2018 Olympic cycle. They had a decent season, ending the year at ninth in the World Curling Tour rankings, but Kevin Koe's team was fourth, and coming into the Brier as the first-ever "Team Canada," Team Morris were not one of the favourites to win.[3] Kevin Koe, Brad Jacobs, Brad Gushue, and Steve Laycock all entered the Brier ranked ahead of them in the World rankings. That was borne out through the first weekend of gameplay, as Team Morris stumbled out of the gate to a 2–3 record. As the story goes, Morris, unhappy with his own play at skip and recognizing that if they didn't make a change, they probably wouldn't win, called a team meeting and told Pat Simmons—the third, who had been a long-time skip for Saskatchewan—that he should take the reins. It turned out to be the right call. The team would only lose one more game throughout the competition, beating Laycock, Gushue, and then Jacobs to claim the Brier crown.

It wasn't just the win either, but a dramatic final shot by Simmons, a draw to the 4-foot for the win. If Canadian hockey players grow up winning the Stanley Cup in Game 7 overtime in their driveways, Canadian curlers grow up dreaming of throwing a draw to the button in the 10th end of a Brier final for the win. Simmons, cool as ever, put it right on the lid, drawing a celebration befitting of Simmons's nature: a broom toss about 25 feet in the air, looking like it had been ejected out of

3 Team Canada, represented by the defending champions, has been a staple of the Scotties Tournament of Hearts for years. They were added to the Brier in 2015 as a way to accommodate each of the three territories—Yukon, Northwest Territories, and Nunavut—getting their own entry, as opposed to being amalgamated into one.

the passenger seat of a James Bond vehicle, and ending up on the sheet beside, which was empty.

Immediately following that, it was just a whole lot of screaming. Lead Nolan Thiessen sprinted down the ice toward Simmons, who, having shed his equipment, had thrown his hands on his head in disbelief. Thiessen didn't care. At nearly a full sprint (not easy to do on curling ice), he picked Simmons up apparently eight feet in the air. That seemed to jolt Simmons awake to his accomplishment, and after sharing equally violent embraces with John Morris and second Carter Rycroft, he let out a series of whoops and fist pumps before finally shaking the hand of his defeated opponent, Brad Jacobs. And perhaps, most fittingly for the final of a Canadian championship, Nickelback's "How You Remind Me" was blaring in the background for some reason. God bless us all.

BRAD GUSHUE

"Mom, answer the phone"

2006 Olympic gold medal game versus Markku Uusipaavalniemi

We now know Brad Gushue as a world-conquering six-time Brier champion who holds a ton of curling records for excellence and will retire as one of the game's greatest-ever players. At the 2006 Olympics, however, he was just 25 years old and had come off one the game's great upsets, winning the Canadian Olympic Trials after making a last-second team change, bringing on veteran Russ Howard to skip the squad and throw second stones, and coming into the trials as one of the lowest-ranked teams in the field. He won, but Canada wasn't sure if he would be the best option to bring home the country's first-ever gold medal in a sport it had dominated for years.

In 2002, Kevin Martin was among the best in the world and the favourite to win gold in Salt Lake City, and he had the chance to do it with a draw to the button, akin to the one Simmons threw to win the 2015 Brier, but he missed it, giving the win and the gold to Norway's Pål Trulsen. Back in 1998, it was Mike Harris who represented Canada at the Olympics, and he also won silver. He had come through the Canadian Olympic Trials process in a similar manner to Brad Gushue, having never won a Brier title before and as one of the lowest-ranked teams in the field. Pundits and fans were worried Gushue might suffer a similar fate.

It wasn't always the easiest path for Gushue either, as he went 6–3 in the round robin, losing two in a row in the middle of the tournament and needing wins in his last two games against New Zealand and the US to guarantee a playoff spot. He got those wins, and then, after a comfortable 11–5 win over that same Team USA to get into the gold medal game, he scored a whopping

6 in the sixth end against the upstart Finnish team, led by skip Markku Uusipaavalniemi, the Curling Spelling Bee's final boss, all but securing the victory. (In case you're wondering, the Curling Spelling Bee begins with *Kevin Martin* and ends with *Markku Uusipaavalniemi*. In the middle, you've got Norway's *Christoffer Svae*, Italy's *Gianpaolo Zandegiacomo*, Turkey's *Uğurcan Karagöz*, Russia's *Nkeirouka Ezekh*, and Estonia's *Kerli Laidsalu*.)

Perhaps it was because he'd taken a huge 10–3 lead in the sixth end, and so had a few ends to think about how he was going to celebrate, but almost as soon as he was finished celebrating with his team, Brad immediately procured a Nokia flip phone from his bag (it was 2006, after all) and attempted to call his mother, Maureen, back home in St. John's, Newfoundland. Using a Nokia phone just after defeating Finland had to have added at least a little insult to injury, but I suppose the country recovered.

When she failed to pick up after a few rings, he looked right into the camera and said, "Mom, answer the phone," and immediately legendary CBC commentator Don Wittman laughed and exclaimed, "Maureen, if you're listening, Brad's trying to get through." It may have been Wittman's encouragement that sealed it, as she picked up the phone shortly after, and Brad enjoyed a moment with her before signing off on the game's final score and doing an interview with CBC, where he broke down in tears while thanking his family for their support. It was the first step in what would become an obsession that Brad's hometown of St. John's had with him, naming a highway leading into the city after him and making him one of the most beloved curlers ever, both on and off the Rock.

SANDRA SCHMIRLER

Seventh-End Surprise

1997 Olympic Trials versus Shannon Kleibrink

If you see a clip of this celebration as part of a highlight package—and if you have watched curling at any point in your life, you absolutely have—you would be easily convinced this was a shot to win the game. Sandra Schmirler, the darling of Biggar, Saskatchewan,[4] was trailing Shannon Kleibrink by one in the seventh end of their game to decide who would get to represent Canada in Nagano, at the first Olympics since curling became a full medal sport.

Schmirler was the overwhelming favourite going into the game, as she was the defending Canadian and world champion, and already had three World titles under her belt at that time. Shannon Kleibrink had only a single Scotties Tournament of Hearts appearance to that

4 Biggar's population is just over 2,000 and has perhaps the most endearing town slogan in the country: "New York is big, but this is Biggar."

point,[5] and was a bit of a surprise finalist, but she had Schmirler on the ropes in the seventh. As Joan McCusker, Schmirler's second, described it, they had missed seven shots in a row, and McCusker had already decided in her mind that they were likely giving up a steal to Kleibrink in that seventh end. But Schmirler, ever the curling brain, spotted an in-off (like a carom in billiards) to potentially score 3. It was an extremely tough shot, one that left McCusker wondering if there was even a shot to score a single point, never mind three of them. Sandra made the shot perfectly, and with the crowd in Brandon, Manitoba, erupting behind her, she lost her mind a little bit.

We do see curling celebrations in the middle of games, but they tend to be fist pumps, hoots, and hollers, nothing that involves a whole team. Not in this case. Sandra threw her broom out of her hands and raised both fists in the air, only to be greeted by McCusker and lead Marcia Gudereit, who had sprinted down the ice to meet her, gathering her in a huge embrace. It looked like they had won the game. They were only up two with three ends to play; this wasn't a shot that had sealed the game. With Team Kleibrink playing as well as they were, it was far from a guarantee. Jan Betker, ever the cool-headed third, went to meet her team, but was a little less keen on

5 The Scotties is the Canadian women's national championship. What the Brier is to the men, the Scotties is to the women.

the embrace, reminding them they still had 24 rocks to throw and nothing was certain.

Funny enough, Shannon Kleibrink did get two points back to tie the game at 6 in the eighth end, but Schmirler was able to put another three on the board in the ninth to help secure a 9–6 win and an eventual gold medal for Canada at those Nagano Olympics. Tragically, Sandra Schmirler would be diagnosed with cancer just a few short years later, in September 1999, and would succumb to her illness in March 2000. It was a huge blow to the curling community, as Sandra was beloved as a player, broadcaster, and person. She has left a beautiful legacy, as the Sandra Schmirler Foundation has raised over $9 million since 2001, to support babies who are born "too small, too sick, or too far" (from the medical care they need). She loved curling and everything about the game, and so it's perhaps fitting that one of her greatest on-ice legacies is a burst of joy that came in the middle of a game, a moment when she was too happy to contain herself, and it lives on in the fabric of our sport.

JENNIFER JONES

"The Best Shot I've Ever Seen to Win a Game"

2005 Scotties final versus Jenn Hanna

Sandra Schmirler died at 36, leaving a lot of questions about what could have been. Even with three World titles and an Olympic gold medal, it felt like there were many more championships in her future, and her death also presented Canadian women's curling with the question of who was next. Jennifer Jones had won a junior national title, but she was 26 in 2000 and had yet to make her first Tournament of Hearts. She finally cracked the national scene in 2002 with her first Scotties berth, but lost in the first playoff round to Sherry Middaugh from Ontario. By that time, she was 28, and while a highly regarded player, she was perhaps not on the radar as someone who might eventually reach GOAT status.

That changed in 2005. Now 31 years old, Jones found herself in her first Scotties final. Playing with long-time second Jill Officer and lead Cathy Gauthier, Jones had added a key ingredient to the mix: Cathy Overton-Clapham at third. The chemistry was instant, and Jones and company made the Scotties final in their first year as a team, facing upstart Jenn Hanna from Ontario, who was six years Jones's junior and sometimes tagged with "the next one" label herself.

Jones struggled in the final, shooting only 70 per cent and trailing Hanna for most of the game. Hanna was leading 6–4 going into the 10th end, and Cathy Overton-Clapham made a critical mistake with her second stone of the end, attempting a takeout on an Ontario stone but instead jamming it onto her own, leaving them shot on the button. After exchanging guards and peels, it came down to the final shot, with Jennifer Jones needing to make an in-off—not dissimilar to the one Schmirler had to make just eight years earlier—for the win. The in-off was made challenging by the fact that the rock she was coming off was quite flat to the one on the button, forcing Jones to throw pretty big weight at it. After commentator Don Wittman set up the shot with Jones in the hack, his colleague in the booth, 1998 Olympic silver medallist Mike Harris, quietly said, "This is so tough." He said what we were all thinking and feeling: that this was a shot Jones makes maybe one out of 10 times, maybe one out of 20. But make it she did, scoring four to beat Hanna 8–6.

The celebration reflected how hard the shot was. Brooms went flying. Gauthier and Overton-Clapham immediately embraced, careful to dodge all the rocks in the house with their feet. Jones, isolated about halfway down the sheet, started screaming and jumping up and down, pausing only to hug Officer, at which point they both started screaming and jumping. Overton-Clapham and Gauthier then found their way to Jones, along with alternate Trish Eck, and more screaming and hugging began. It was then that Harris uttered the words, "That's the best shot I've ever seen to win a game." Most people tend to agree, calling it the best shot not only in Scotties history, but in the history of the game as a whole. It is so revered, in fact, that it is often simply referred to as "the Shot."

And my favourite part of the entire celebration? When Jennifer Jones's dad, Larry, who was their coach, comes out to hug Jennifer, and then the team realizes they have yet to shake their opponents' hands. Because the coaches' bench is positioned behind the sheet, often the pattern in a championship game is to celebrate with your team on the ice, shake the hands of your opposition, and then make your way off the sheet to the carpeted area behind, where you meet your coach and your fifth. The team realized that if Larry—now hugging Jennifer—had made his way to the middle of the sheet, something had upset that balance, and enough time had elapsed that he figured he couldn't wait any longer to join the celebration. As the camera shows them hugging, you hear a voice say, "We have to go shake their hands!" They then bound immediately to the other end of the ice, where the disconsolate Team Hanna shook their hands, and then they continued the celebration anew. A shot that good deserved an extra moment, but the spirit of curling can never be broken.

HONOURABLE MENTIONS

You didn't think I would leave you with only five epic celebrations, right? Here are some more:

KAYLA SKRLIK

ScreamFest 2023

2023 Alberta Scotties final versus Casey Scheidegger

Kayla Skrlik had been poised to break through in Alberta for a while, and after running through the field undefeated, including a win over Casey Scheidegger earlier in the tournament, she needed a very precise, thin double takeout on her last in 10th to get the win. After she makes it, the entire team erupts in shrieks normally reserved for a broken leg or a Taylor Swift concert, with teammates Geri-Lynn Ramsay and Skrlik's sister Ashton flinging their brooms into space and turning to scream in Kayla's direction with a force reminiscent of Chuck Yeager breaking the sound barrier for the first time. If reading this makes you want to go and seek out the shot on YouTube—and you should, the shot is amazing—make sure you turn the volume down.

KEVIN KOE

The Frog Hop

2017 Roar of the Rings final versus Mike McEwen

Putting a Kevin Koe celebration after the Kayla Skrlik one is a lesson in contrasts. Kevin Koe is a stoic man. A man of few words who took his elementary schoolteacher's advice about using his indoor voice much too literally,

Kevin isn't really one to celebrate. He's had some big wins over the years, but he tends to let the celebrations happen to him, with other teammates getting far more excited. But when he won the Canadian Olympic Trials in 2017 on a draw to the 4-foot, he leaped roughly one foot off the ice surface, hands and legs splayed, and let out a "*Woo!*" For Kevin Koe, that was the equivalent of bungee jumping from the rafters in his underwear, and it's still one of my personal favourite celebrations for that reason. Don't worry: after a big hug with second Brent Laing, he pretty quickly composed himself and went back into Koe Mode. And as a bonus, this celebration also included one of the longest broom throws in history, as lead Ben Hebert showed he might have a future in the sport of underhanded javelin, tossing his broom the entire length of the ice sheet in ecstasy.

BENOÎT SCHWARZ-VAN BERKEL AND PETER DE CRUZ

The Chopper

2010 World Junior final versus Ally Fraser

As you might imagine, the unbridled passion of youth lends itself to some great celebrations, and this one might be the best at that level, as a home Worlds in Flims, Switzerland, led to a victory for the Swiss team led by skip Peter de Cruz and fourth Benoît Schwarz-van Berkel. Although a lot of celebrations happen because of a made final stone, this is the rare one that happens owing to a miss. Because misses in curling hit so hard and we've all been a part of them, most of the time, a team that wins as a result of their opponent's missing doesn't celebrate much until they've shaken hands with the other team, and even then, there is a subdued air to the proceedings. Not so here, as Ally Fraser misses the final stone for Scotland, and Schwarz-van Berkel goes in for the hug with de Cruz, who immediately picks Schwarz-van Berkel up and begins spinning him around, his legs flailing in the air like the blades of a helicopter. Schwarz-van Berkel looks to be about a hundred pounds soaking wet, and after de Cruz puts him down, he immediately collapses to his knees in disbelief over the victory. Although the Swiss pair would eventually win an Olympic bronze medal, it's too bad we never saw them win another big championship, as fans would've loved to see a repeat of the helicopter when they were older.

MATT DUNSTONE

The Yard Sale

2013 Canadian Junior final versus Thomas Scoffin

Matt Dunstone has become a household name in the curling world over the past few years, losing Brier finals in 2023 and 2025 and consistently being ranked near the top of the sport. But back in 2013, when he was just a scant

17 years old and, as he later told me, didn't even know how to spell *curling*, let alone play it at a competent level, he won the Canadian Junior Championships in exciting fashion in his first trip to the big dance. He was facing Thomas Scoffin in the final, one of the Yukon's finest-ever curlers, who had been to the Canadian Juniors in the five years previous, and had moved down to the University of Alberta to grow his game. He was also a Youth Olympian and had won a bronze medal at the 2012 Games a year before, so he was the favourite going into the gold medal game. When Dunstone made the final shot for the win, a cheeky little in-off to splash a bunch of rocks in the house and leave himself lying one, he acted as surprised at the win as the viewers at home may have been. An expression of disbelief etched across his face, Dunstone began a series of leaps that were so powerful that his corn broom just flew out of his hands. He put both his hands on his head, and it was there that his "MB" hat lost its grip on his flowing salad.[6] He then finally made his way into the house, embracing third Colton Lott with such a fury it nearly knocked them both over, and the picture of Dunstone celebrating, his broom suspended in the air like a magic trick, has lived on in curling memory ever since.

6 My editor informs me that the hockey slang *salad* for hockey hair has not made its way to the mainstream, so let's see if this book helps/hurts.

CHAPTER 8

CELEBRATE GOOD TIMES... OR NOT

As we have discussed, curling is a sport that has a lot of downtime built into it. Things don't often happen instantaneously, and thus, strangely, there is a history—albeit a somewhat brief one—of celebrations going wrong. There are two in particular that stick in the memories of curling fans and will forever live in infamy.

Of course, celebrations can be premature in other sports too. Egos can get the best of players, or some sort of rules review can call a winning goal or winning play back against a team that has already celebrated. But in the history of curling, there have been two distinct moments when celebrations actually worked against a team—one that perhaps teased the karmic gods too closely, and one when the celebration cost the team a game they would have otherwise won. Oh, and that game was the World Championship final.

But first! We head to 1985. I've heard a lot of rumours that 1985 was a great and special year, particularly for adorable and promising newborns. That year also saw Pat Ryan and Al Hackner face off in the Brier final, and the last two ends of that game have been stamped into curling history, so deeply that when Netflix made a show about famous sports losses called *Losers*, they included this game and its loser, Pat Ryan, in the show. As a full episode. I know that may not sound like much, but any sort of *Wide World of Sports*–type program almost never features curling. It was big for us.

PAT RYAN

Doubled Down

1985 Brier final versus Al Hackner

Curling is often thought of as an old person's game, but in reality, the top competitors are often on the younger side. In 1985, there was no exception, as two of the game's rising young talents, Alberta's Pat Ryan and northern Ontario's Al Hackner, 29 and 30, respectively, faced off for Canada's—and curling's—biggest prize, the Brier. Both were entering the final with some history on their side. Hackner had won the Brier three years before, in 1982, at just 26 years old, one of the youngest skips ever to do so. Pat Ryan's history was a little bit more recent—he had run roughshod through the field at the Brier, sporting a perfect 11–0 record heading into the final, with his team of Gord Trenchie, Don McKenzie, and Don Walchuk,[1] including a win over the Hackner rink in the round robin, 5–3.

The two were a study in contrasts: Pat Ryan had the swagger and attitude of a young athlete. He had a swooping haircut, a tightly groomed mustache, and look, I'll just say it: he was a handsome guy. The way he carried himself on the ice suggested that he was better than you, and he knew it. He was also a singer, just as comfortable whipping out an acoustic guitar and belting one out around a bonfire or onstage as he was stepping out onto the curling ice and kicking your ass. Curling probably doesn't have "jocks," but if it did, Pat would be wearing a letterman jacket.

Across the sheet from him stood Al Hackner, every bit the opposite. He was nicknamed the Iceman for how calm and collected he was out on the pebbled sheet. He wore gigantic glasses, which were the style at the time, but also you kinda felt like they would be his style at any time. He looked like a guy you would ask to fix your computer. Not now, but in 1985, when no one even had a computer. He drove trains for CN Rail, but you would

1 Yes, it's not lost on me that there was a curling team consisting of a Pat, two Dons, and a Gord. They probably deserved to be Team Canada just based on their hoser-rific names alone. Oh, and their alternate? He was also named Don.

100 per cent believe he also designed them and figured out how they ran and also probably had a model train set in his basement. It was a classic battle of brains versus brawn, though Ryan was mighty smart too. This is chess on ice we are playing, after all.

The final was playing out almost exactly as Ryan wanted it to. In the days before the free guard zone, if you were a good hitting team and could get an early lead, you were very tough to beat. Pat Ryan was both very good at obtaining an early lead and very good at hitting, so he won a lot of games. Things were playing out very similarly to their first meeting, with Ryan leading 5–3 heading into the 10th and final end. In their round-robin match, Ryan's team was able to keep the house virtually devoid of any Hackner stones, and Hackner didn't even throw his last stone, with no opportunity to score two. Ryan probably envisioned the 10th end of this game unfolding in a similar fashion, and if it did, the Brier championship would be his. As for Hackner, all he could do was throw guards and pray for a Ryan miss. Hackner's lead, Pat Perroud, threw up a corner guard and those prayers were immediately answered, as Don Walchuk, perhaps under the pressure of the moment, flashed his takeout attempt. Hackner was in business.

After exchanging some further guards and hits, Ryan decides to draw one into the house to count one and force Hackner to bring play to the middle of the ice. Rick Lang,

Hackner's third, tries a freeze on that Alberta stone, but taps it into the back 8. That leaves enough separation for Ryan to peel it out, and Alberta ends up lying two—the rock in the back 8 that Lang tapped, and Ryan's shooter, which rolls to the outside 12-foot. Hackner decides to play a split so that he can get two of his rocks into the rings and perhaps give himself a shot for three and the win if Ryan were to miss. He makes it, but Ryan is still counting one at the back of the house.

And then karma calls, and Pat Ryan picks up the phone. Pat immediately looks at hitting the outside one of the two that Hackner has just split. He believes that if he makes the hit and roll to lie two, Hackner will be left with almost no shot, and he'll win the game. It's not an easy shot—few shots have been played on the outside of the sheet, and there's a guard in the way. It seems most likely that he'll make the hit but not the roll, and give Hackner a shot for two. But this is Pat Ryan. He is 11–0 and at the time maybe the best individual shotmaker in the world. He makes the shot perfectly, rolling in toward the 8-foot, and he believes he's won the game. He immediately raises his arms above his head, and then brings them down on top of his head. He can't believe it. In his mind, he's won the Brier. In fairness to Pat, it's in other people's minds too. Lead Don Walchuk does a little jump and raises his broom in the air when the rock comes to rest. Commentator Don Duguid, himself a three-time Brier champ, remarks on Ryan's celebration and says, "It seems as though Pat Ryan has realized he's just won the Brier!" The crowd is going crazy. Al Hackner does not appear fussed.

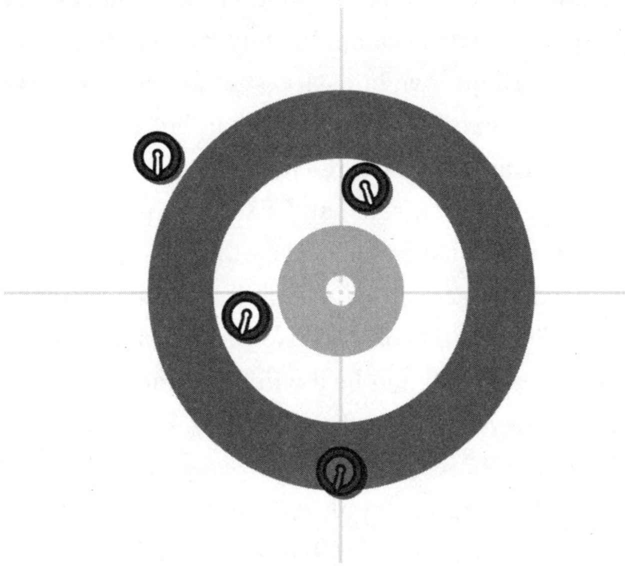

Duguid believes Hackner has only one option: to run his own guard back and attempt to make a very thin double takeout—*thin* meaning you'd almost have to miss the first rock you're hitting in order to execute the double. Hackner has other plans. These days, we are used to championship ice curling a great deal: anywhere from four to six feet. In those days, ice-making techniques weren't as advanced and rocks just didn't curl that much.

Maybe two to three feet at best. For all intents and purposes, it looks as though the rock Ryan has just thrown is too far gone behind the guard, and even if you make it by the guard, the double is incredibly thin. Duguid describes it as a "one in a thousand" shot. Hackner seems to like those odds.

The sweepers barely touch it. That's perhaps what's most notable about the shot to me. Most of the time, a crucial shot is going to have some measure of sweeping involved, but this moment is too pure for that. Hackner makes it almost by himself. He gets by the guard, hits a kitty whisker of the Ryan shooter, and rolls onto the back one, tapped there by Rick Lang what feels like an eternity ago. Duguid immediately loses his mind. "*Can you believe it?*" he screams over the inferno that has just erupted in the crowd in Moncton, New Brunswick. "*I said it was one thousand to one, and he made it!*" Al Hackner is stoic as his team celebrates. It appears as though his heart rate has never risen. He has scored two, and we are going to an extra end.

To Pat Ryan's credit, after the din dies down, he slides to the other end with Hackner and congratulates him on the made shot. Hackner touches Ryan's shoulder, almost in consolation, both for what has transpired and what is about to come. You see, when the dust settles, Pat Ryan is still a massive favourite to win this game. He has the hammer in an extra end, in a game with no free guard zone. He likely wins in this situation 90 or 95 per cent of the time. But karma isn't finished with Pat, and after Gord Trenchie crucially flashes a peel halfway through the 11th end, Hackner gets in the driver's seat. He forces Ryan to a difficult draw to the 4-foot, and Ryan misses, perhaps still shook from what happened just 10 minutes before.

They would call it "the Shot" in the years that followed. As we know from the previous chapter, that moniker was taken by Jennifer Jones's in-off to win the 2005 Scotties 20 years later. Although it's tough to say which shot was harder—they both had extreme difficulty, even if one in a thousand is hyperbole—Jones's shot was to win the game, and Hackner's was just to tie. If Pat Ryan doesn't miss the draw in 11, we would still talk about how good the shot was, but it would always come with the knowledge that it was in a losing effort. We now simply refer to it as "the Hackner Double." I like that. Al should own the shot, even 40 years later. It was that good, even if I'll spend my life wondering if the Pat Ryan celebration caused it.

BOB LABONTE

The Curse of the Boot

1972 World final versus Orest Meleschuk

Watching the 1985 Brier final feels like stepping into a different time: grainy TV footage; curlers wearing big, bulky sweaters rather than streamlined athletic wear; feathered haircuts. If the 1985 Brier final feels like a different time, the 1972 World final feels positively Jurassic.

First of all, the smoking. Despite curling's 27-years-and-counting dalliance with the Olympics, the increasing strength and professionalism of the athletes, and its overall sex appeal,[2] the average person still thinks of a curler as slightly overweight, maybe balding, and definitely holding a beer. Well, imagine that, but you could also smoke on the ice while you played. Throughout the 1972 World final, both skips are chain-smoking, making shots to try to secure the world championship with long, ashy butts hanging out the corners of their mouths. Ashtrays are not only at both ends of the rink for the skips, but even midway down the sheet for the sweepers. Both teams are wearing flared pants, and both teams have haircuts that appear to be straight from *The Outsiders* movie.

The 1972 World final was unique for a few reasons besides cigarettes. Canada was represented by Orest Meleschuk, a curling lifer who was widely respected but only made the Brier out of his home province of Manitoba twice: in 1972 and 17 years later, on the back end of his career, in 1989. The United States was represented by an equally unlikely crew of four, who were all university students and 22 years of age or younger. They showed up to many of their events wearing gold pants, which drove the curling establishment crazy.

By that time, Canada had won 11 of the first 13 World Championships, and so Meleschuk was the favourite before the event started, simply by the colour of the

2 Seriously. Curlers are young and hot now. There's even a yearly charity calendar that features curlers in various states of undress.

sweater he was wearing. And heading into the gold medal game, he had done nothing to dissuade anyone from the notion. He had stormed through the round robin 7–0, scoring at least eight points in every game he played and breaking double digits in four of them. He had also beaten LaBonte in their round-robin meeting, 11–1. The United States had only one curling gold to its name at that point, won in 1965 by curling legend Bud Somerville. It seemed highly unlikely that this team of young upstarts was going to dethrone the Canadians, 10 years their senior and in prime position to capture the country's 12th championship.

But things were not going according to plan. Meleschuk had jumped out to an early 5–1 lead, but the US put a ton of pressure on Canada in the second half of the game, scoring six straight points across three ends to lead 9–7 heading into the final end. Meleschuk would need two to tie and three to win, neither seeming impossible, given how many points he had scored throughout the tournament. But curling is a game of momentum, and he didn't have a ton of that heading into the critical 10th end.

Heading into skip stones, Meleschuk was actually set up to score three, but LaBonte made a slick double takeout on his last and rolled onto the button to lie shot, forcing Meleschuk to make a hit around a guard to lie two and force an extra. Meleschuk came barrelling out of the hack, cigarette dangling from his lips, sideburns twisting in the wind, and while he did make the hit, he didn't hit it right on the nose, and the rock began to slide slowly out of the 8-foot. He needed to remain in the full 8-foot to score his two, and US third Frank Aasand started to sweep. With the corn broom slinging, Aasand appeared to have moved the rock far enough out of the 8-foot. Meleschuk had only scored one, and the US had effectively won the game.

Now, here's where I must discuss rules with you. I know, it's boring, I'm sorry. It'll be quick. When all the rocks come to rest after the hammer stone, you must confirm with the opposing third what is happening in the rings, in the same way that you sign your opponent's scorecard in golf. Typically, the third of the team that has scored will say something and/or make a gesture to their opponent about how many points they have scored. When—and this is important, *only when*—the opposing third has confirmed the score can you submit the score to the scorekeeper as official.

Back to the game. Aasand sweeps the rock out of the 8-foot, and he looks down at his stone. He looks down at the Canadian stone that Meleschuk just threw. He goes wild. He has seen with his own eyes that they have won, but it's close. Close enough that the other third would want to take a look at it to confirm it, especially considering this is the World final. As Aasand jumps up and down, skip Bob LaBonte, who was previously standing a few feet behind the house, assumes that it is obvious they have won, and he begins to jump. Unlike Kevin Koe's frog hop, LaBonte is going for it. He is jumping as high as he can, and his arms are outstretched, and he is jumping on ice. Curlers spend a *lot* of time standing and moving around on ice. We can generally handle jumping on it. But at perhaps the worst possible moment, LaBonte cannot.

As he lands, his gripper gives way and he falls, kicking Meleschuk's stone that had just come to rest. He falls almost cartoonishly, like he has slipped on a banana peel. It makes the clip even harder to watch. And when I say *kick*, I mean kick. It moves at least four inches. Meleschuk's third, Dave Romano, hasn't even remotely had a chance to look at how close it was to confirm that it was indeed only a score of 1 for Canada and, therefore, a US victory. LaBonte removes the cigarette from his mouth angrily[3] and is forced to concede that because Romano didn't have a chance to look at it, the Canadians earned the point. And much like the 1985 Brier final, despite having the hammer in the extra end, LaBonte cannot convert on it, and Meleschuk will be crowned champion.

It is heartbreaking to watch. It's heartbreaking to even think about: a moment of joy—the greatest joy

3 I'm not joking. Curlers were literally just smoking out there. All the time.

in sport, becoming a world champion—that actually changed the result of the game. It's like hitting a grand slam to win the World Series and then missing the plate—something so outlandish that it doesn't even seem possible in a game being played on the sport's greatest stage. But there it was for all to see on the German mountainside, and now on the computer I carry in my pocket.

The only cool thing to come out of that? Al Hackner got the Hackner Double and Bob LaBonte got what was referred to as "The Curse of LaBonte." As I stated previously, Canada won 11 of the first 13 World Championships, and made it 12 of the first 14 with Meleschuk's win. But then, out of nowhere, Canada wouldn't win another world championship for eight years. In the ensuing period, the United States would win three, in 1974, 1976, and 1978. And where did Canada win the 1980 World Championship? In Moncton, the same building where, five years later, Pat Ryan would raise his arms in fateful triumph and Al Hackner would bury him with the Shot. I love symmetry.

As for the Curse of LaBonte? It may have worked for those eight years, but the curse has been on the United States ever since. As of this book's publishing, the 1978 win by Bob Nichols is the last time a US men's team won the world championship. Canada went on to win 24 more.

CHAPTER 9

THE WORST LOSS EVER

I lost a lot.

In sports, even serial winners win only a little bit more than 50 per cent of the time—they just win the right games at the right time (or make the right shots at the right time, though I suppose those are one and the same thing). For there to be serial winners, there needs to be serial losers, and I was one of those. I figured it was important after writing four thousand words about two of the most dreadful losses in the sport's history that I give a little bit back to you, the reader, and to the Pat Ryans and Bob LaBontes of the world by telling you about *my* worst loss ever.

In Pat Ryan's case, he's probably doing just fine. After that loss to Al Hackner, he went on to win the Brier three times and the Worlds twice. He also narrowly missed out on qualifying for the Olympics when curling was a demonstration sport in Calgary in 1988. He parlayed his success in regular men's play to a Senior Men's title as well, besides having a great run as a coach. He also played in 10 Briers and never had a losing record in any of them.

As for Bob LaBonte, making the World final when you're 22 probably leaves you thinking you're going to make a lot more of them, but he never did. He never managed to win even the United States title again. It just goes to show how difficult a sport curling is to win consistently. For every Pat Ryan, there's a Bob LaBonte. But hey, at least Bob got to taste national championship glory and a World silver medal. For every Bob LaBonte, there's at least 50 John Cullens.

I probably should have quit.

I didn't know it at the time, but my loss in the 2001 Juvenile Regional Playdown final was a harbinger. I was only two years into my curling career, I was 15 years old, and I should have quit right then, after the worst loss I've ever had. It's a loss so enduring that it can defeat almost any other "worst loss" story at any table of curlers. As we've established, curling is a very social game, and as we also know, misery loves company. The only thing better than sitting around a sticky curling-club lounge table after a big win is commiserating with all your friends about your big loss. Everyone in curling has a big loss, but mine tends to trump everyone else's. So let me tell you about it.

First things first, and I grant you this: the stakes were relatively low. Yes, when I was 15, it was the biggest game I had played in up to that point, but the loss cannot stack up to losing a World final on a technicality or celebrating early in a Brier final. In my career, I did go on to win seven medals at various BC provincial championships, but none of them are gold. There are people with resumés much more devastating than that, losing double or triple the number of provincial finals I did, or losing multiple Brier finals (sometimes in a row), or any number of losses that mean an awful lot more than some kids losing out on a provincial berth at the U-16 level.

But in terms of the scoreboard itself, and taking the stakes out of it, it is tough to find a loss worse than mine, even at the absolute lowest levels of the game. I'm sure there's a rec-leaguer or two out there with a similar story, but there aren't many. So let's go back to the beginning.

I grew up a hockey player. My first season of curling happened mostly because it did not conflict with hockey. The junior curling program at the York Curling Club ran on Sunday mornings, and my hockey team that season never had games or practices on Sundays. The two commitments coexisted in easy harmony. Two hockey practices a week, two hockey games a week, and then a blissful Sunday morning spent in the cozy York Curling Club, playing two curling games as part of their junior league, which was a great way to learn the sport. This was in 1998. I was in Grade 8 and preparing to attend Newmarket High School the following year, I was playing rep hockey, I was getting into curling, and life was good. And then my father made a proposition.

He had received an offer for a transfer to Vancouver, British Columbia. He was a branch manager of an insurance adjusting firm, and they needed a new man out west. At the time, my dad had built one of the most successful offices in the country in Newmarket, and figured if he applied for the job, he would get it. After he consulted the family, we agreed we would support the change. Sure enough, he got the job, and in 1999, we headed out west, none of us having even visited Vancouver before. It ended up being a great choice for me personally, as I thrived in a new city and a new environment, and it also led me to get much more seriously into curling.

As any good Canadian knows, hockey is our official winter sport. And it is also rife with politics. There is something about being an undeniably good hockey player that does guarantee success, but for every kid that earned it on their own merit, there are another five whose dads are friends with the coach, or engaged in some light bribery, or bought an entire junior hockey team so that their kid could play on it, or in some cases even 90 minor hockey teams and a scouting service.[1] This isn't a book about hockey, so if those sentences offended you, don't worry. I'm just a lowly curler. But hockey politics did, in some way, lead me to curling.

When we left Ontario, I was playing rep hockey. Rep hockey is shorthand for "representative hockey," meaning you play for your hockey association against other hockey associations. You have to try out and be selected for a rep team, as opposed to houseleague, where you are simply assigned to a team within your association and play against other teams in that same group. Put simply: if you are good, you play rep, and if you are not, you play houseleague. I had played rep for most of my childhood. But moving across the country to a new town and being a new face does not lend itself to getting onto a rep hockey team, even if you're good. Rosters and reputations are already established from years of playing within the same association. It's very hard to be the new guy on the block. After we loaded our stuff onto the moving truck, one thing we brought on the flight across the country was my hockey equipment, so that I could try out for the rep

---

1 If you're not Canadian and this sounds made up, I assure you that it is not. Stuart Hyman, father of Zach Hyman of the Edmonton Oilers, at one point owned over 90 teams in the Greater Toronto Hockey League, probably the most prominent minor hockey association in Canada. He said it was for the greater good of hockey, but it probably didn't hurt his kid's chances of making it either.

teams in my new city. I was summarily dismissed after just two tryouts. I hadn't played houseleague in years, and I was confused as to why I wasn't given more of a chance. Maybe uprooting a teenager's entire life and having him try out for a rep team where no one knows him, two days after a cross-continent flight, had something to do with it. I'm unsure. But in any event, I didn't want to play houseleague. What I did want to do was play curling. So I quit.

I know that quitters never win, or whatever else a hockey team paints on its dressing room wall for inspiration, as if that makes a difference, but I just had this nagging feeling. It wasn't so much that hockey wasn't for me anymore. I still loved the sport, and do to this day. I still play recreationally and on outdoor rinks. No, the nagging feeling was that curling could be my thing. It had so many things I liked about it, and quitting hockey just gave me the push I needed to make it my full-time deal. I was so used to the gruelling minor hockey schedule, with multiple practices and games every week, that putting all that energy into curling made me feel like I could go somewhere, and quickly.

Luckily, the Peace Arch Curling Club also saw that in me. Although the PACC didn't boast the massive junior program of the York Curling Club, with its 20 teams that could compete against each other every week, it did have two things: a group of kids very willing to play and learn, and a great coach willing to teach them.

Jack Tucker had gone to the Brier a couple of times, representing BC, and was also a pilot whose initials were JET. In short, he was cool for an older fella, and a damn good curler. He was also very interested in giving back to the game that had given so much to him, and very quickly fell in love with the team of misfits that we put together.

Given our ages (I and two of the other team members were 15, and our skip was 14), playdowns—tournaments where you try to earn the right to qualify for the provincial championships—weren't even on our radar. We began practising together and playing in our local junior league, but that was about it. Back in those days, each region was granted a spot at the juvenile playdowns, which were U-16. It was our coach who signed us up. I don't remember, but I think I didn't even know what playdowns were. I figured it was just another bonspiel (our fancy word for "curling tournament," which, funny enough, is just the German word for "tournament." I probably wasn't even aware of the implications of what a provincial was, who made it, and why it was such a big deal.

But just as I would be for any bonspiel at the time, I was excited for two reasons: the first was that it was an opportunity to curl. Back then, I loved and was grateful for any time I could get out on the ice and play. Once I figured out that making the provincial championships was indeed a big deal, I was excited for that too. But I was also excited because I had absolutely zero expectations. I was playing third at the time, and my skip, Jeff, and I were the only two players on our team who had curled for more than a year. Our second and lead were both first-year players. There was simply no way we were going to win this, or even get close, and there's something about that feeling as an athlete that was very freeing.

We made the final. I don't remember how, and quite frankly, were it not for the outcome, I probably wouldn't remember the game itself either. All I know is that we weren't expected to be there, by ourselves, our coach, or anyone else.[2] The fact that we had even made the final was astounding to us, but now that we were there, we thought, why not win?

We were up against the Miller brothers and their stalwart team from the Valley Curling Club. If you know any curlers, you're probably aware that most curlers

---

2 In fairness, our coach was frequently bearish when it came to our odds. A couple of years after this, we decided to enter the Peace Arch Men's Bonspiel, a tournament open to all ages and skill levels. We were joking around at practice one day about winning the whole thing, and he told us to temper our expectations and that if we won even two games, he would take us out to dinner. We won the whole thing. He took us out to dinner *and* a movie. That movie? *Men with Brooms*. Not even joking for the purposes of this book. Timing is everything.

start curling because their family curls. Many top curlers will share stories about how their parents took them to the club as a toddler and let them ride on top of the rocks and used the friendly confines of the club as a free babysitting service. That was the Miller brothers' story. Their parents curled. There were the two of them, and they also had two sisters, and they all curled. Their dad was their coach. They expected to be in this game, and they expected to win it.

No one on my team had a parent who curled. We all found our way into it by being huge nerds and bad at everything else. All right, I was okay at hockey. The rest of my team—well, let's just say they were a little less athletic. Our parents tried their best to get into the game once we got into it, but certainly they weren't ever going to be coaching us, or even knowing what was going on. My mom was a classic "hockey mom," always cheering me on at my games and encouraging me and my teammates. She wanted to do the same thing for curling but didn't understand the rules, so after I completed a shot, sometimes I'd slide down to the other end and she would give a thumbs-up through the glass, and I would have to give her a thumbs-down, letting her know that it was actually a pretty poor result.

And so it was that we were heading out onto the ice, us a ragtag outfit of four guys who had met each other just five months before, and our opponents a band of brothers, ready to fulfill the destiny set forth for them at a young age. They had already been to juvenile provincials once before, the previous year, which had had the bonus of coinciding with the BC Winter Games as well. Every two years, athletes from across the province would gather for this Olympic-style event where you won medals both for yourself and for the area of the province you were from. Everyone I know who has gone has said it was one of the more memorable experiences of their lives. That wasn't on the line for us in this game, but the Millers had that experience the year before, and were ready to take in another provincials experience in 2001. If you were a betting person putting odds on the game, we were probably a +750 underdog. Maybe even more. The Millers had already beaten us handily once in the event, and there was simply no reason to expect they wouldn't do it again.

If we were a +750 underdog just to win the game, I'm going to go ahead and guess that the odds were significantly more astronomical that we'd be ahead 8–2 after six ends. And you know what? I have absolutely no idea how we got there. I can't tell you the exact line score, I can't tell you about any big shot we made to put a big score on the board that helped us build that lead, nothing. The funny thing about painful memories is that they often start right when the pain begins and leave you unsure of what came before. Now, not being able to remember it might also have something to do with the fact that it was 25 years ago, and I have played many, many curling games since. But I'm gonna go with the pain thing. That's more poetic.

I shouldn't say my memory starts in the seventh end, because that wouldn't be true. It actually starts just before that. But first! A rules detour:

1. This curling game was scheduled for eight ends. Although most playdown games are 10 ends, it was considered a little too taxing for kids aged 16 and under to be playing 30-end marathons on three game days. So we were up 6 with two ends to go.
2. Curling teams can concede the game to their opponent at any time. While many sports fans are familiar with the term *garbage time*,[3] most often associated with football but with other sports as well, curling has no garbage time, because if we're getting beat too badly, we put that time exactly where it belongs: in the garbage. You are allowed to just grant your opposition the victory if you don't think you have a chance of coming back.

---

3 Garbage time is the time when a game is clearly out of hand but the rules state that every game must be completed—as when one football team leads another 35–7 with five minutes left in the fourth quarter. It is most often used in fantasy football, where "garbage time touchdowns" can occur that have no bearing on the result of the game itself, but the scores the individual players get for fantasy purposes can have outsized results on fantasy matchups.

My memory starts with the end of the sixth end. We scored however many points it was to go up 8–2, and our opponents went to concede the game to us, offering to shake our hands. Before our palms could touch, the Millers' coach, their dad, banged on the glass from the curling club lounge and called a timeout. At the time, coaches were only allowed to call a timeout at the juvenile level. Something about kids needing to learn the game. At all other levels, timeouts had to come from the players themselves, on the ice. If we had been playing at any other level, this game would have been over and you wouldn't be reading about it. But alas, he called a timeout and gave the kids a fairly valuable (and obvious) message: This is the final. There are no games after this. This is also juvenile curling—momentum swings are a feature and not a bug. You might as well keep playing. And who knows, maybe he also threw in something about how we were clearly the worse team and probably didn't even deserve to be in the final against them. I don't know. But in any case, the timeout ended and they elected not to shake our hands, and the game continued.

But, of course, we were young teenagers, and this was sport, and there was pressure. They were visibly upset. Even though they had received the pep talk from their coach-dad, it didn't seem like the Miller brothers cared a whole lot about playing out the string. Perhaps, instead of experiencing their loss any longer out in the cold ice shed, they would have rather been inside the warm confines of the curling club lounge, consoling themselves with a hot chocolate. Well, luckily for them, we chose precisely that moment to forget everything we ever knew about the game (which, as I've laid out, wasn't much). We couldn't stop missing. I don't know if the reality finally sank in that maybe we were actually going to win this game and go to provincials and the stakes all of a sudden mattered, but we were shook. We gave up four in the seventh end, and now led 8–6.

Any good curling team will tell you that a two-point lead with the hammer is more than enough to win the game. The stats at the highest levels of the sport will say there's actually a 90 to 95 per cent chance. In normal circumstances, even after giving up four the previous end, you'd still favour your chances to win. You keep the house clean, make a few shots, and given you have the last stone, you'll probably have a shot to win. But we were young, and not that good. We did not keep the house clean. I don't remember any shots from this game except two. The first is the other skip's last shot in the eighth end. There were a ton of guards in play, and we were sitting one on the button with a few of our rocks and their rocks scattered around. There was no easy way into the house, and so the older Miller decided the only way they could score two points (and remember, we still had to miss) was to try an in-off, similar to the one Jennifer

Jones would make five years later (with the stakes much, much higher).

An in-off is a very hard shot at any level, but it's even harder when you're 15 years old. You're just trying to get it somewhat close and hoping for the best. I have a vivid memory of the stone travelling down the ice, and he was sure he had missed. A look of great pain began to cross his face, and even though I didn't know much about curling, I knew we were going to win. But then, seemingly out of nowhere, it curled. His face went from pain to jubilation in about four seconds, as he made the in-off, and when the smoke cleared, they were lying two. We were blown away. I went from thinking we wouldn't even have to throw our last shot to realizing, suddenly, that the pressure was once again entirely on our shoulders. We had a couple of shots to potentially remove a Miller stone and win the game, but they all came with risk. We might actually remove one of our own stones and give them a score of 3 and the win. Knowing that the odds were still in our favour, we decided to throw the rock away, giving them two, a tie, and head to an extra end.

By now, you have probably figured out how that went for us. It went from 8–2 and 95 per cent of a concession to 8–8 and an extra end. Again, the percentages will tell you that a top team with the hammer in the extra end of a tie game still wins 70 to 75 per cent of the time. But the percentages now truly didn't matter. We were a group of

14- and 15-year-olds who had felt the pressure of curling for the first time, and we were not equipped to deal with it. We did have a shot for the win, but it was a tricky hit that needed to evade a couple of guards on the way to the house, and we did not make it. We just tipped the guard, and they won the game 9–8. Seven points in three ends to beat us. It was astonishing.

I remember that I wasn't too upset once the game was over. I certainly wasn't happy, but I didn't know enough about curling yet to know how truly devastating this loss was. Plus, I agreed with my parents, who assured me after the game that hey, I was 15 years old. There would be many more big games in my life, and many more chances to win them. In theory, they were right. But in 25 years of practice, they ended up being dead wrong.

I should have quit.

That drive away from the Langley Curling Club should have been the last drive I'd ever take away from an ice shed. But I am stupid and curling has addictive properties. I would be back. In fact, I would be back in the same building one year later, when something almost more devastating would take place.

CHAPTER 10

THE WORST WIN EVER

WARNING: This chapter contains graphic descriptions of the rules governing regional curling championship qualification. Reader discretion is advised.

So yeah, I lost a game 9–8 after being up 8–2 with only two ends to play. That was very unfortunate, but as I explained before, we weren't supposed to win that game anyway. It was our first year as a team, and no one on the team had more than two years of curling experience. It was fairly easy to shake off that loss, despite how punishing it was, and to recognize that there were many good years ahead of us. The following year, however, in 2002, we won a game that might actually have been more brutal than the one we lost the year before.

!!RULES TALK!!

The BC juvenile championships operated on a two-year cycle. One year, the winners of their respective zone playdowns would go to the BC Juvenile Curling Championships. The next year, the winners would go to the BC Winter Games. Then, the next, it would revert to the BC Juvenile Championships, and so on, and so forth.

Back in the halcyon days of curling, when participation was running wild and kids didn't have phones and therefore needed something to do, BC curling was actually not one united organization as it is now, but was split into two organizations: the Pacific Coast Curling Association, which covered the Lower Mainland and Vancouver Island, and the British Columbia Interior Curling Association, which covered everything else. Each organization was then divided into regions, and the associations decided how their regional playdowns would translate into berths at provincials.

I grew up in the Lower Mainland, BC's most populous area, and my association also included Vancouver Island, so we had a ton of regions—11, to be exact. Often, in those days, my regional playdown would consist of three different regions: 8, 10, and 11. The number of berths at a provincial championship from those regions often varied based on participation, but it was usually one berth per region, for three berths at the provincials total. However, in 2001, a BC Winter Games year, one of the regions had zero teams register. So it was determined by the PCCA that the losers of the Region 10 and Region 11 finals would get a second chance at making the BC Winter Games, and have a one-game playoff for the vacant Region 8 spot.

!!RULES TALK OVER!!

With that regional-final loss in 2001 in our back pocket, we actually felt as a team like we were onto something. We also got the bonus of a new teammate, Sean. He was both a curler and a competitive speed skater, and was a boon to our team. At the time, our curling club had two junior boys' teams, an older, more experienced one and ours, which was younger and newer. Sean was a member of the more experienced team and had one more year of juvenile eligibility left, and so, because of our relatively great result the year before, he joined our team for the playdowns. We felt really good going into the playdowns, as we practised a lot more, started playing in a men's league at our home club, the Peace Arch Curling Club, and really just dedicated a lot more time to the sport.

We were ready to head back to the very same Langley Curling Club, which was hosting the playdowns again, and we were ready for another try. There was one problem, however. The Miller brothers were both still eligible for juvenile provincials, and they had added some new blood to the squad. Two of their team members had aged out of juveniles, and they solved that problem by absorbing half of the top team in the region next door. They were essentially a powerhouse, combining forces like the geeky, teenage Avengers reboot we never got. We were still just four guys, none of whom had more than three years of curling experience, and with this new combination, we had no chance.

Although the Millers' other teammates had given us a chance to be up 8–2 with two ends to play, there would be no such flirtation with disaster this time around. It was a double knockout and we lost to the Millers twice, and the dream of representing our region was over. However, that second game was indeed the final, and by virtue of losing our regional final, we were going to play off against the Region 10 final loser for that vacant Region 8 spot. In fact, we even conceded that final against the Millers early. We learned no lessons from the year before, when they had come back on us, but that was okay, because we were saving our energy for this second chance at winning a regional spot and a trip to the BC Winter Games.

We headed into the final against a team we had played and beat before, and we were confident. With this new-look lineup that featured Sean and had me, Justin, and Jeff with another year of experience, we knew this was a game we could win, despite even those losses to the Millers. And win it we did. Comfortably, in fact. I don't remember the score, but I do remember we didn't even play the eighth end. Everything my parents had told me the previous year had come true. I just had to be patient and keep practising, and there would be so many good years and good wins ahead of me. This was just the start.

I was 16 years old, I had been curling for only three years, and I was heading to the BC Winter Games, one of the pinnacle sporting events that a teenager can participate in. Not only that, an added bonus: this was a Canada Winter Games year. Every fourth year, much like the Olympics, the Canada Winter Games happen. If your parents happen to time your birth correctly and you're a little closer to the U-18 cut-off of the Canada Winter Games, you could win your province and get the prestigious invite to the CWG—a chance to meet kids from across the nation playing your sport, and establish yourself as a player to be reckoned with for the future. My parents had gotten everything right, and they definitely knew back in 1985 that just 16 years later we would move 3,500 kilometres away and I would get the opportunity to compete at a BC Winter Games, and maybe a Canada Winter Games too! Having grown up in a small town in Ontario that was never particularly good at hockey, this was the biggest sporting win of my life.

It's hard to imagine a time before smartphones, when every move of a child's life wasn't documented, but there are very few pictures of me curling at this time. There is one that persists though, one that still exists in family photo collections. It's a photo taken directly after this game. It's of me, Jeff, Justin, and Sean, all holding our "zone winner" badges with emphasis toward the camera. We are wearing ill-fitting clothes, none of us have grown into our faces yet, but you can tell: we are extremely happy.

I hate to dampen this story, I really do. I hate to dampen it both for you, the reader, who I hope, after living through the previous chapter with me, is cheering me on. I also hate to dampen it for myself. I'm not a "time machine" person and I don't live with a ton of regrets, but if I could go back to any moment in time, this would make the shortlist. I also hate to dampen it because, as you may have discerned from this chapter title and the general theme of my entire curling career, this story does not have a happy ending. And it doesn't have a happy ending because of *rules*, which is the worst kind of unhappy ending possible.

The protocol followed in the playdown we'd just been through at the Langley Curling Club would have been correct if this had been a year when there were no BC Winter Games. In such years, if a region has no teams signed up to compete, other regions are allowed to battle it out for the empty spot. But this was a Winter Games year—and unbeknownst to us, in a Winter Games year it is the host region that gets to fill any empty berths.

I know. That stabbing pain you're feeling right now is the same one I had at the time and as I'm writing this. In the age of the non-ubiquitous internet and in a sport almost exclusively run by the senior set, the person in charge of our playdowns did not think to check that ruling. *He held a playdown for a spot that did not exist.* And the worst part is, he did not find this out until three days after the games ended. I'm assuming he called up Curl BC, told them that he had the three selections for the BC Winter Games from our zone, and was then informed that actually, no, it was the local boys from Williams Lake who would be getting the spot.

I had three full days to daydream about going to the BC Winter Games. I had other curlers who had experienced it tell me all about it. Getting to meet athletes from all across the province. Getting to meet girls from all across the province. Spending time in a new community, getting a chance to travel for curling, this new sport I had fallen in love with, and getting to represent my region at a provincial championship alongside hundreds of other kids from my area, all working toward the same goal. The Winter Games are a big deal, especially to a kid. Opening and closing ceremonies. The whole nine yards. And that Canada Winter Games berth was also on the line. I got to go to Tuesday night men's league and have all the adult curlers I looked up to congratulate me on winning the spot. My parents had started to make travel arrangements for them and my sister to come and watch too. It was a really great three days. And then my coach called.

He was nearly in tears. As I said before, Jack was a cool guy, but he was also a very sweet man. And very competitive. He wanted this as much as we did, and he was truly heartbroken to have to break our hearts. He said that the regional representative was very apologetic and couldn't believe he had made this mistake. Jack did say, however, that we would be recorded in the BC curling annals as having won the zone, and we would be able to keep our zone winner badges. As you may imagine, that was a very, very cold consolation. I felt like the kid at the end of the classic children's book *The Hockey Sweater*. I mostly just wanted to take my curling jacket, with the zone winner badge stitched on, down to the local church and pray for a thousand moths to come and eat it.

Once again, my parents had the same message. I was still only 16 years old, after all. And I was technically a zone winner. I was on the right track. There was still a long way to go in this game for me, and there would be many more big games to play in, and to win. They might've even taken me to Boston Pizza to cheer me up. That's a pretty good parenting move. A spicy perogy pizza can cure a lot of ills. There are always lessons to learn in life, and curling has taught me many lessons along the way. But I should have learned one lesson the game was telling me as soon as I got off the phone with my coach.

I really should have quit.

All right, all right, I know. I've been a little heavy on the "I should've quit" stuff. Obviously, I am glad I never quit curling. I have loved the game pretty much since the first time I ever played it, and I stayed with it far longer than any of the teammates I brought up in the previous chapter. All of them, to a person, quit by the time we were done high school. That was never going to be satisfying for me, and I ended up sticking with the game at a highly competitive level until I "retired" at age 34 to take up my second life in the sport as a media personality, which is going far better than the "playing" part ever did. But it's probably important to note that I did play for a long time and I was pretty good at it.

In the years after the stories you've just read, I did pretty well. I made it to 11 BC Men's Provincials in a row, medalling six times (two silver, four bronze). When I was a kid in high school and would do those "goal-setting" things they make you do as part of your academic path or whatever, one of the non-academic goals I listed every time was making the Brier. Those two silver medals mean that I was one win away from the Brier twice. Not bad. I lost a BC Mixed Provincials final, too. I was really good at winning silver medals throughout my time. But I did win some tournaments too: somewhere between seven and ten World Curling Tour events of various prestige and prize money, which meant my team was good enough to peak at 25th in the world and around 20th in Canada. By virtue of being ranked around 20th in Canada, my team was about three-to-five teams away from making the Olympic pre-qualifier a couple of times. Also not bad. And I won my fair share of Coleman camping lanterns and toasters, and one time, at a junior bonspiel, I even won a pager and a free year of service. It was the year 2000, so I assure you, that was a big deal back then, even if no one ever called me and I literally never used it. However, you bet your ass that for that entire year I had it clipped to my belt as a status symbol. Pretty cool stuff.

CHAPTER 11

MY FAVOURITE END EVER #2

Martin versus Murdoch, 2009 World Championships Final, 10th End

In 2006, Kevin Martin wanted to win, and he wanted to win badly. World championships had eluded his grasp. He had sat out a few Brier championships in a row to help support the fledgling Grand Slam of Curling, and while that ended up being a daring and critical move for the health of the sport, he was forced to watch his provincial rival Randy Ferbey pick up four Brier titles in five years while he sat on the sidelines, twiddling his broom. The curlers had been fighting with Curling Canada over the fact that the Brier was a championship where no one won any money, and sponsors were not allowed on jackets. The Brier was making Curling Canada millions, and the curlers saw none of it. As one of the biggest names in the sport and a huge ticket draw for the Brier, Martin knew that if he sat out, Curling Canada might eventually capitulate, and he was right. They did, giving money to

IF I DON'T SHOOT
WHAT DOES HE DO?

every participating team in lieu of sponsorship, and tens of thousands to the teams making the playoffs.

Martin was a Canadian Junior champion, a multiple Brier winner, and an Olympic silver medallist, but he knew that to reach the pinnacle, he needed to do something different. He was about to turn 40, and he recognized the game was changing.[1] It was getting stronger. It was getting more technical. And perhaps most importantly, it was getting younger.

It was not uncommon over the years for older skips to pick up younger players. It helped bring new players into the game's elite tier, while giving the older skips some fresh blood, from both a strategic and a strength perspective. Kevin Martin had even done it himself, bringing Carter Rycroft, 11 years his junior, into the fold in 1999. What was uncommon was to construct a team on which every player was much younger than you. You needed veteran wisdom, veteran talent, guys who had been there before and done it all. That was the conventional way of thinking, and it had worked for a long time. Well, Kevin wasn't interested in conventional thinking, and he had a secret weapon: John Morris.

---

1 In curling, turning 40 is not a death sentence, as it is in other sports. Some might even argue that skips don't truly get good until their 30s, meaning that turning 40 can serve as a halfway or three-quarter point in a player's career. We don't have a midlife crisis in curling, only a midlife celebration.

John Morris was in a similar boat. As a skip himself, he had won two World Junior titles and made a couple of Briers during those fallow Grand Slam years, even losing a final. But he knew he needed to do something different to get to the top of the mountain. A chance meeting with Kevin Martin at a Canada Cup led to a conversation about how the two of them had something in common: a strong desire to be on the No. 1 team in the world, to be in the conversation among the game's top players, and to be winning those huge championships that had eluded them in the past.

They both knew it required some sacrifice, both on and off the ice. John was proposing bringing in two players even younger than himself: Marc Kennedy and Ben Hebert. John was 12 years Kevin's junior, but Marc and Ben were both born in the 1980s. They had been in high school when Kevin turned 30. They were listening to Pearl Jam, and Kevin thought that was something you put on toast. They were just in their mid-20s and only starting to grow into their curling careers. They didn't have the resumés of Kevin's past teammates.

Ben had won a World Junior championship, but it was as an alternate. Marc had never won a Canadian championship and only had one Grand Slam title to his name. It was a huge risk for Kevin, who could have picked up older teammates who had not only that veteran experience but maybe a little bit more in common with Kevin, who was married with kids, owned his own business, and had seen and done just about everything in curling. Plus, he had to learn a bunch of new slang words, and if the team stunk, that would not be radical or coolbeans at all. It was a huge risk for his three young charges because they were betting they could have chemistry with the Old Bear, and could make a team arrangement like this work even though it had been rarely seen in curling's past.

In their first year as a team, they won the Alberta championships and made the playoffs at the 2007 Brier. The next year, they went undefeated through the field at the Brier and only lost one game at the World Championships, defeating Scotland's David Murdoch in the final for the first world championship for all four team members. They were also running roughshod over the Grand Slam of Curling, winning five titles in their first two years as a team and making the finals in two others. They were the World No. 1 with a bullet, and went undefeated again at the 2009 Brier, setting the stage for what looked like a second consecutive World title. They had reached the heights they had set out for themselves just a few years earlier, and were now hoping to climb even higher, as if Mount Everest had a secret second summit when you got the top that was just beckoning to have the Canadian flag planted on it.

The only thing standing in their way on the international stage was David Murdoch. Scotland is the birthplace of curling, and Murdoch wasn't about to let Kevin Martin have his way with a sport that was first played on his country's frozen lochs. Murdoch was no slouch in the curling world. By the time the 2009 Worlds rolled around, his resumé was deep. He had won a World title just a few years before, in 2006. He had also won three European Championships, and was a two-time World Junior champion. He had also lost the 2008 final to that same Kevin Martin rink, after defeating them earlier in the playoffs. He had the pedigree to beat Kevin Martin, but, perhaps most importantly, he wasn't *scared* of the Canadian rink.

Back in those days, I was just getting my own feet wet as a competitive adult curler, playing in some of the same tournaments that these two rinks were playing in. Although I never matched up against either one, we did note that in those days, a lot of teams paid what we called the "Kevin Martin tax." With the Martin team being so dominant both on tour and on the world stage, it was not uncommon for teams to be flat-out afraid to play them. Knowing that they were so good, teams would frequently take improbable risks or try too hard when faced up against Team Martin, and often ceded big ends to them early. You would often look around while out on the ice to see that, yes, again, Kevin Martin had scored four in the first end against some lowly local team made up of farmers and accountants. These days, the top teams are all very good and play each other so often that this phenomenon is much less likely to occur. But back in those days? It was an honour just to be nominated. And crushed. But hey, maybe Kevin Martin would buy you a beer in the curling club lounge after he beat your ass, and that was a story you could tell your grandkids.

Murdoch, though? He was one of the best in the world. He was unbothered by such things, and Team Martin would have been well aware that they needed their best game to beat him. In fact, at the 2009 World Championships, by the time the two teams made it to the final, Murdoch had already beaten Martin twice at that tournament. He beat him 6–5 in both teams' last game of the round-robin portion, and then immediately beat him 7–5 in the first game of the Page playoff.[2] After winning the semifinal, Team Martin set up a rematch with Murdoch in the final, hoping to end the tournament with

---

2 Ah, the Page playoff, one of curling's favourite tournament-organizing tools. For those unfamiliar, a round robin is played with each team playing every other team in the competition. In other tournaments, you might see the semifinals composed of the No. 1–ranked team playing No. 4, and No. 2 and No. 3 playing each other. Not so for "Pip" Page, an Australian rules football delegate. Of course it's an Australian guy who invented it. Anyway, I digress. No. 1 plays 2, 3 plays 4. Winner of the 3-4 game moves on, loser is out. Winner of the 1-2 game gets a bye to the final. Loser of the 1-2 game plays the winner of the 3-4 game in a semifinal for the right to play the 1-2 winner in the final. Easy. Simple as, is what an Australian would say.

a 1–2 record against the Scots, which in this case would be, improbably, good enough to be crowned back-to-back world champions.

We could dig into the particulars of the game, but this is an essay about my favourite *end* and not my favourite *game*, and so we must skip ahead, once again, to the 10th end. For the non–curling fan, there are exciting ends that happen outside the 10th end—and there are also exciting first halves of basketball games, but no one talks about those when someone makes a buzzer-beater. And what makes this game so special, so memorable, so talked about, is not a shot that was made, but rather a shot that was purposely thrown away. It's as if a basketball player had a contested look with one second left on the clock in a tie game and decided they might be better off not even trying to shoot and going to overtime instead. It's a decision that now, even 15 years later, gets debated in curling club lounges around the world. But first!

The game is tied 6–6 heading into the 10th end, a fitting score given how closely these two teams are matched. Barring something extremely wild, this will be the final end of the game. Someone will score here, and they will be crowned world champion. I should say, I suppose, that something extremely wild *does* happen, but it isn't a blank end. We will declare a winner.

We are in the sold-out Moncton Coliseum in New Brunswick—home turf for the Canadian team, but not so far from Scotland that Murdoch and Co. feel completely isolated. In fact, Moncton is actually closer to David Murdoch's home club in Lockerbie, Scotland, than it is to Kevin Martin's in Edmonton, so vast is Middle Canada. But make no mistake, this crowd wants Kevin Martin to win. The 2010 Olympics are less than a year away; they are also in Canada for the first time in 22 years, and we look like we have the answer to cracking the podium in this foursome from Alberta's capital.

Scotland throws up a centre guard with their first stone, and Ben Hebert, crucially, misses the tick.[3] Now, that miss is not crucial to Canada's success or lack thereof—in fact, it's Hebert's only miss of the game—but it is crucial in setting up the story that's about to unfold. That miss allows Scotland to get two guards up on the centre line, and we have ourselves the potential for an exciting end.

With Marc Kennedy's first stone—the first of the end in which they are allowed to remove the guards from play—the team makes a big decision: they will not remove the guards from play. With an opportunity to hit-and-roll underneath the guards looking too juicy, the

---

3 Remember how I told you about that "free guard zone" earlier? Hebert cannot remove the rock from play, but he can "tick" it off of the centre line, moving it toward the side of the sheet. This keeps the centre line and, most importantly, the button open for Team Canada, who only need to score one point to win.

team decides to have Marc play that instead. I wonder if they regret this decision now, never mind the one to come later on.

After a Scottish draw, Canada does finally decide to chase the double peel, but John Morris misses, peeling only one of the two guards. This leads Scottish third Ewan MacDonald to throw a small tap on the only Scottish stone in the rings, leaving Canada still lying two, but the situation near the button is getting a bit more complicated. John Morris then peels the second Scottish guard, and something magical happens.

Looking to play another tap, David Murdoch throws his first stone a little wide, kissing off the Canadian stone and then leaving his two Scottish stones lined up on the Canadian stone on the button. It was a miss, but not a horrible one, and it leaves the Scots in a decent position.

The way the angles line up, Canada isn't sure of their options. There are a few potential hits available to clear some stones, but they're worried that a slight mis-hit in any direction would leave Murdoch the opportunity to put the screws to Canada and give them no shot on their last one. When you have the last rock in a tie game in the 10th end, the last thing you want when you get into the hack to throw that last rock is to have no available shot. After the Scottish stone comes to rest, Kevin Martin and his squad of young stallions begin to discuss what to do. And after one minute and 45 seconds of discussion,

Martin tells the team to hold on a second, and then utters these fateful words: "If I don't shoot, what does he do?"

If I don't shoot. What. Does. He. Do.

Eight words that a skip almost never utters, and definitely not on their first stone, and definitely not in a tie game in the last end of the World Championships. There are generally two instances when a curler would purposely throw a stone out of play. The first, and most common, is when a lead throws their first stone or two of an end through the rings because they have such a commanding lead that putting their stone in play can only help their opponent generate offence. The second is when a skip surveys the house on their last stone and realizes there's nothing they can do with that stone to improve their situation—and that in fact it may make things worse—and so they throw it away. Most skips would never consider throwing their first stone away. But most skips are not Kevin Martin.

The team calls a timeout, and Kevin's words, initially, are ignored. As veteran coach Jules Owchar, looking as though he just crawled out of bed, ambles his way down the side of the sheet to have a talk with the team, the other three players are still discussing various options, all of which include hitting something in the rings. The angles are complicated. Jules arrives, and Kevin asks Jules what he thinks they'll do if Kevin doesn't throw. Jules isn't quite sure. The team continues to talk. They take the second of their two timeouts. Curling teams almost never take two timeouts consecutively. In other sports, taking two consecutive timeouts is illegal. The team is paralyzed by their own decision-making with the World title ominously hanging in the balance.

Kevin then asks Marc what he thinks they'll do if Kevin doesn't throw. Marc, 27 years old and now a world champion, but still on some level just thrilled to be playing with Kevin Martin, says, "I don't know, Kev. You know more than me."

He then slides down to the other end, perhaps realizing that Kevin does know more than him and probably anyone else in the world at that time about the game of curling. Kevin says one more time, "I'm thinking of throwing mine through, actually." Ben Hebert, quiet for most of this exchange, immediately says, "I don't like throwing it away," and offers two options he prefers.

At no point during this now *five-minute* team exchange does John Morris ever concur with Kevin that throwing it away is the shot. He continues to press for more options. Even the crowd, watching a World Championships final with two teams in the heat of crunch time—presumably, the scenario they dreamed about when they shelled out for tickets—begins to grow restless. They don't have the advantage the home audience does of hearing the curlers miked up, painstakingly discussing every option, none of which they seem to like.

The crowd starts doing the wave. John, recognizing they will have to make a final decision eventually, directly asks Kevin, "What do you like?"

Kevin responds, "Throwing it away!" with the fervour of a child pushing a food they don't like off their high chair.

Finally, mercifully, after now six full minutes of discussion, John acquiesces. "I don't mind it, Kev." Ben Hebert immediately reacts: "You're serious?" Kevin says yes, and begins to slide down to the other end, and the scenario he saw in his mind four minutes ago plays out. He throws the rock away. The sound you hear is armchair skips across the country knocking their beers over in disbelief. No one has done this before. Kevin Martin, perhaps already envisioning the headlines calling him a genius for making this choice, cedes control of the house back to the Scots, with nothing disturbed. This end has now hit the 20-minute mark, inching toward the longest end in curling history played against time clocks.

Dave Murdoch almost can't believe his eyes. If someone watching at home is surprised, imagine being across the sheet from Kevin. He doesn't seem excited, necessarily. It's probably something like the feeling of playing a board game you haven't quite grasped the rules of, against your neighbour who has a room in his house dedicated to Dungeons & Dragons. *Is he just that much smarter than me? Is there something I'm missing?* Sure, curling has been described as chess on ice, but you'd never see Garry Kasparov figuring his best move isn't to make one.

Weirdly, it probably helps Scotland that they don't have much time left on the clock. There isn't enough time to consider if they're being punk'd or not. They have about 90 seconds in which to make their decision and throw the stone, and they decide to play a quiet weight hit that removes the yellow stone closest to the button, with their rock spinning atop a Canadian stone. It's the shot they wanted to make, and it puts pressure on Martin, but even still, when the camera pans to Murdoch after the rocks come to rest, he looks confused. He still isn't sure if this is real life, and if he's being subjected to some master plan he's about to become aware of in the next minute or so, once Martin goes to throw. He looks like he's wondering if the call is coming from inside the house, and Kevin Martin is hiding in the attic, ready to drop the final stone on his head.

Luckily for Murdoch, none of that is true. If it's a master plan, it isn't a very good one. If Kevin Martin is in the attic, the floorboards underneath him are starting to creak. The shot he's been left with is much more difficult than Martin imagined. He has to play a double takeout where the margin for error is very slim. Most likely, if he'd known that throwing the rock through would make the shot this hard, he would've thought of something else.

Hindsight is always 20/20, but that hindsight doesn't often come mere minutes after the event in question.

He misses the double. Sliding a little tight, the rock never gets to its intended target, and David Murdoch wins the game and his second world championship.

Make no mistake, had Kevin made that final double, we would have called him a genius. And he was, and is, one of the best curling minds to ever play the game. Losing this game didn't change that. It's why his team trusted him. It's probably why he trusted himself. Curling is like chess in many ways, but the one key way in which it's not is that there's an infinite number of moves. The pieces aren't fixed. Situations can arise that you have never seen before, and even the most stalwart minds can be challenged by the angles and the rock placements that come up in a game. Lots of curlers make the wrong choice lots of the time, but most aren't good enough to be granted the privilege of doing it in a World Championship final, seen on TV by millions and second-guessed by just as many. Privilege, or curse. Maybe both. Maybe that's why we continue to let ourselves be tortured by this beautiful game.

A quick postscript: while this end is magical and displays the razor-thin margins between victory and defeat in our sport, I recognize a lot of this chapter focuses on the negatives for Team Martin. But two positives did emerge from this loss.

The first? Marc Kennedy told me in an interview once that he thinks without losing this game, they wouldn't have gone on to win the 2010 Olympic gold medal in Vancouver. Spoiler! Less than one year after the most crushing defeat of their careers, Team Martin reached the pinnacle of the sport in a once-in-a-lifetime opportunity to clinch gold on home soil, doing it on the second-to-last day of competition to set up the win by the Canadian men's hockey team and Canada's record for most golds in one Winter Games. They needed something to reenergize them, give them more motivation, and let them know they weren't infallible. It worked. They went undefeated at the Olympics (including a win over Team Murdoch) in a tournament performance many think is the best of all time by an individual team.

The second? If Kevin Martin had made his last shot, skips everywhere from beer league to the top of the World Curling Tour would've strongly considered throwing the rock away as an option when it probably wasn't. Feelings were spared. Teams were spared. A slew of "geniuses" were not created overnight, and we do have to thank the final missed shot for that.

CHAPTER 12

IT'S CALLED CURLING FASHION, LOOK IT UP

When you hear the word *curling*, a lot of things may come to mind. *Sport*, *winter*, *Olympics*, *drinking*, etc. I'm willing to bet that in a game of word association with *curling*, one word that would take quite a long time to come up is *fashion*. But the sport's fashion does have a long and interesting history, and I think that's for a few reasons.

The first is that there are no "franchises." In the Big Four sports, in soccer, in rugby, you name it, you have long-established teams that have logos and uniforms that have been there for decades, maybe even centuries. Players have no say in their design (generally), and they don't tend to be recycled, except in soccer, where jerseys are a global fashion statement and there's a lot of money in creating new ones.

Curling has no jersey-selling money to speak of. If teams make money off branded items, it's almost always

a T-shirt or a hoodie, and not an on-ice uniform. This is because there's largely no practical use for them. Curling teams today wear jackets, short-sleeved shirts made of some kind of performance material, and athletic pants. It's not a fashion statement to wear any of these things other than to curl, and so they're difficult items to sell.

The other unique thing about curling uniforms is that they are almost exclusively designed by the teams themselves. The only exception to this, generally speaking, is when a team represents their country at a Worlds or Olympics, or their province at a Brier or Scotties. In those cases, the uniforms are designed by their respective sport federations, or whichever clothing company has the Curling Canada contract, in the case of the Brier and Scotties.

One thing curling does have in common with other sports is that the fashions have changed over the years as the sport has become more athletic, and as we've learned a lot more as a society about which materials are best to play sports in. Just as hockey used to have big, bulky sweaters and football players used to wear something akin to a burlap sack as pants, curling has undergone a lot of fashion changes over the years to end up where we are today. As someone who became known on the internet as "curling's fashion expert" and who has long considered how important the general fashion of the players is to the overall perception of the sport, I'm here to rank all the major curling fashion choices throughout history—14 of them, to be exact. While we may not have the diversity of choice that other sports have, we have had some iconic looks, and I'm here to tell you which ones were the best, and which ones are most certainly better left in the past.

14. GIGANTIC PANTS

Era: 1995–2007

Look. We were all wearing stuff that was way too big in the late '90s and early '00s. At the risk of sounding like Grampa Simpson, it was the style at the time. Giant jeans, huge sweaters, T-shirts that came down to your knees—these were all on offer, and I wore all of them and thought I was cool doing it. Where you didn't see a ton of baggy clothes was in sports. Golf had its "baggy shirt" period (seriously, go look up some of Tiger Woods's early wins—he's drowning in his Sunday reds), but for the most part, sports require some level of aerodynamics. Going baggy can mean too much resistance from the wind, water, or whatever other force may be acting upon an athlete. As you may guess, that is not an issue in curling.

What is an issue is how dreadful these things looked, and there's no more egregious example than Jennifer Jones at the 2005 Scotties. We will be watching the shot she made to win for the rest of time, and no matter how many times you watch it, she is still wearing those ridiculously oversized pants that flare out almost from the hips, cutting a very odd shape around the legs. In Jennifer's defence, this was not her fault. At the time, Scotties teams were outfitted head-to-toe by the sponsor, Scott Paper. These days, curling teams are permitted to wear whatever pants they want, so long as they're matching. But at that time, Scott wanted a uniform look, and so they gave you the pants. And none of them fit. And they were made by...

13. PACE SETTER

Era: 1990–2006

If you are not a curler and reading this book, have you heard of Pace Setter clothing? Of course you haven't. No one has. As far as I can tell from a cursory search of the internet, they were a clothing company that started in the late 1970s, based in Winnipeg, Manitoba. Specializing in track jackets and other athletic wear, they got the contract to outfit teams at the Brier and Scotties starting in 1990, and held it for 16 years, which is an unfathomable amount of time in the sporting world, where apparel deals change hands constantly. How and why they got a stranglehold on curling, I don't know, but usually in these situations, it's a somebody-knows-somebody–type thing. I just wish they knew somebody who knew how human bodies are shaped.

Pace Setters never fit anybody. Even in an era when clothes were designed to be baggy, these things hung loosely from every body part, looking like a ripped grocery bag clinging to a tree branch. Everyone who wore one looked like they were 20 pounds heavier than they actually were. And there's no chance they made specialized women's sizes; if a woman laid flat on her stomach while wearing a Pace Setter, she looked like she might drown in it. For 16 years, our national championships at almost every level of the game were outfitted by this company, and it might have even contributed to the way curling was perceived by the general public as unathletic and homely.

The best part? Some of the provincial associations bought a bunch of theirs in bulk, I guess cutting a deal with Pace Setter, which doesn't seem smart in retrospect. But hey, when a company is in charge of the national clothing for 16 years, maybe you figure another 16 are on the horizon. So what happened was that for other national championships where you weren't required to wear a specific brand—like your junior nationals, your mixed nationals, etc.—those provinces had to send players in Pace Setters *well* after the baggy-clothes trend was over and they were no longer outfitting the Brier and Scotties teams. Tough break.

12. MATCHING JACKET-PANT SET

Era: 1980s

As stated above, women's curling had a very tough time with fashion, and one of the moves that the national championships made in the '80s was to give female curlers a new look by matching their jackets with their pants. As with the Pace Setters (and a lot of these were also made by Pace Setter), the clothing was provided to the curlers, and so nothing fit properly. It also just didn't look good at all. In other sports, pants are made to match the tops, and this looks fine, but there was something about curling that made it all look quite amateurish. Given that there isn't a need for aerodynamics (or even for going out of the way to make players/teams distinctly identifiable, since they aren't wearing any equipment), it never really made sense and never really fit the game. Oh, and there was the whole thing where a bunch of the teams were given white pants to wear, and they were completely see-through. One team even went so far as to buy underwear with hearts on it to fit the Scotties vibe and because they knew the fans were gonna see their underwear anyway. Not ideal.

11. TOO MANY BADGES

Era: 1970s–1990s

For a time there, curling got very obsessed with badges. Since the dawn of the Brier, teams were given a very beautiful crest to put on their sweaters, shaped like the purple-heart logo of Macdonald Tobacco, the first sponsor of the Brier. It has since become one of the more iconic symbols in the game, with "getting a Purple Heart" becoming synonymous with "making the Brier," one of the highest achievements in our sport. And you don't even have to get shot to get one!

The symbol was so effective that it's now used across all Canadian championships, with the Scotties having a red heart, seniors getting a golden one, etc. That crest, however, made every curling association in Canada and around the world think that everyone should get a badge for everything. When I won that zone title in the last chapter? Badge. Win your region? Badge. Make it to provincials? Badge for getting there, plus sponsor badge. For a while, curling even had a badge program like swimming, where you would get a badge of a certain colour, shaped like a maple leaf, to denote your achievement. You'd have 12-year-olds whose curling jackets weighed more than they did.

Teams would carry their jackets over from year to year, and that led to the badges stacking up—it even became a trend at the Brier, where accomplished curlers would have the Purple Hearts up and down their sleeves. Although it was a unique way to show off your accomplishments, it also made all the jackets look horribly tacky, and it would weigh them down. Curling has smartly switched to giving the curlers their Purple and Red Heart badges framed, while sublimating (printing directly onto textiles) an equivalent onto the jackets. And you don't get a badge for making a takeout when you're nine years old anymore, which is also a positive.

10. GOLF SHIRTS

Era: 1970s–1990s

It is not an accident that almost everything on the list here is the result of the national association outfitting all the teams at the Canadian national championships, and this was another episode. In the older days, teams could do whatever they wanted for shirts underneath their bulky sweaters (we're getting to those). You could have a crested T-shirt, a polo, whatever you liked, as long as it was of a matching colour and design. Curling Canada put a stop to that in the '70s by introducing golf shirts to the equation. Don't get me wrong, nothing wrong with a good golf shirt, but these shirts were heavy, they were bulky, and in an era before athletic fabrics, you can imagine golf shirts did not have the *best* material to stitch or iron on letters or crests. So you'd often have the shirts match in colour, but the letters would be all over the place, like alphabetic fridge magnets that had just been attacked by a toddler. It got fixed a little bit more in the later '80s and '90s, when you could make golf shirts out of a lighter cotton and transfer the letters and crests on better, but for a while there, it made curling look amateur. Which I suppose it was. But making the Brier was a huge feat and the gentlemen there could've looked more dapper than they did.

9. WHITE BELTS

Era: Team Howard, '00s

There have been some team-specific fashions over the years that we won't detail here, but this one is worth a mention because it actually inspired quite a few teams to do the same. Most curling teams wear black jackets and black pants, but when Glenn Howard represented Ontario often at the Brier in the '00s, he wanted to do something to stand out, and he chose white belts. It isn't entirely his fault. We had a true "white belt" era in the early '00s when we thought it was a good idea to give the drummer from blink-182 his own clothing label and companies whose sole marketing strategy was "put these clothes on an MMA fighter" emerged. It probably shouldn't have trickled down to curling, but Glenn had two twentysomethings on his team in Craig Savill and Brent Laing, and so it was that fortysomething Glenn Howard showed up on the scene wearing all black with a white belt, like he was auditioning to be an extra in a My Chemical Romance video.

At the time, it was funny, and it worked. The juxtaposition of "old guy tries modern fashion" is usually a hit. But looking back, it's tough to say it was a good look. The big belt buckle with a curling rock on it was also emblematic of the time, and didn't help.

8. NECKTIES

Era: 1920s–1970s

As I've stated repeatedly, the advent of athletic wear—and the evolution of curlers as athletes—has really made the clothing better, both to look at and to play in. But back in the day, before the widespread use of nylon and Lycra and other blessed products, athletic wear was nowhere to be found, and curling was "the Gentleman's Game," after all. And what does a gentleman wear? Well, a tie, of course. There are tons of old pictures of curlers wearing their bulky sweaters (yes, yes, we are getting to that) and underneath, they're wearing a collared shirt with a necktie. As a look? I love it. It gives all the photos a "time and place" to them, but unlike the white belts, it looks sick as hell and has aged beautifully. But as someone who curled for 20 years in the modern era, I cannot believe anyone ever played while wearing a button-down shirt done all the way up to the neck, and a tie. It seems supremely and insanely uncomfortable, and starchy. Much, much too starchy.

7. KILTS

Era: 1600s–1990s

The sport of curling originated in Scotland. I can neither confirm nor deny that the players were wearing kilts back then, but I think it's safe to assume. They probably looked pretty cool doing it. That extended into the 20th century, when curling started to get a bit more competitive and a bit more global, and men still wore kilts and it looked cool. What I like less is that one of the predominant early fashions in women's curling (and remember, women's curling hasn't been around *that* long; their first world championship wasn't until 1979, a full 20 years after the men's) had them also wearing "kilts" (really, they were skirts), with long stockings or nylons underneath. It was not a good look.

It really felt like a relic from another age, when it was fine to allow women to have their own world championship as long as they played in skirts. It got worse as time went on, and it really felt like the options for women were either giant pants that were very unflattering, white pants that were see-through, or a skirt. Eventually, the sport grew up, we got some clothes that actually fit, and we haven't seen a kilt on the ice in high-level competition since the early '00s. This ranking is an amalgamation of Scots wearing kilts on-ice in the Shakespearean age (good) and women having to wear them in the '70s (bad).

6. TAM-O'-SHANTERS

Era: 1600s–1950s

A perfect complement to the kilts, tams were very popular headwear in curling from the game's early days through to the mid-1900s. It is not uncommon to see pictures from that era of four guys wearing the goofiest hats possible while being some of the best curlers in the world. It's beautiful, and I think the hats being ultimately a little bit silly-looking fits the vibe of the sport incredibly well. No notes.

5. BELL-BOTTOMS

Era: 1960s–1980s

Curling has rarely been in line with fashion trends in its lifespan as a competitive sport. The one exception seemed to arrive not necessarily because a collection of curlers decided to follow the latest and hippest thing, but mostly because, without athletic wear or stretchy pants, bell-bottoms actually allowed the best and most comfortable slide.

The curling "long slide" delivery, where the curler takes off from the hack and holds on to the stone until somewhere between the top of the house and the hog line, was popularized by curler Matt Baldwin in the 1950s. Before that, a curling delivery was mostly one motion: you pushed out of the hack, and as you were pushing out, you released the stone, barely hanging on to it. Realizing he had better control over weight and line when he held on to the stone for longer, Baldwin began using the long slide and then won four Briers in five years, from 1954 to 1958. Curlers everywhere began to copy Baldwin's style, but even for Baldwin, the long slide likely demanded finding some accommodating pants. If you've ever seen a long-slide delivery before, you know: it's deep. It's like a forward lunge, but even deeper. Some curlers have most of their body almost touching the ice as they slide. Starchy pants in the 1950s weren't going to get it done.

Curlers are generally pretty smart people. I'm sure that once bell-bottoms arrived on the scene in the '60s, it didn't take them long to connect to the fact it might be nice to have a little more room in the knee and the lower leg as they were sliding. And so it came to be that many top curlers of the time began to use bell-bottoms on the ice, and I'll be honest: it looks cool as hell. The pants flaring as you slide down the ice, the combination of curling's modesty with the bell-bottom style leading to very muted checkered patterns on an otherwise fashionable pant—it all works for me. The pants were so effective for the long slide that curlers were using them well past their expiration date as a popular fashion item, which also contributes to curling's overall aura and makes me love them even more.

4. THE NASCAR ERA

Era: 2000s–present

I don't think I'm saying anything surprising here, or speaking out of turn, but curling is... Well, it's not exactly a rich sport. Although the game itself has become increasingly professionalized over the last two decades, the money has yet to catch up, and most curlers try their best to be "professional" at it while having some kind of side hustle in the off-season, or during the season, or at all times. Some curlers are substitute teachers.

Some have very understanding day jobs that allow them 15-plus weeks of vacation a year. Some are caddies at St. Andrew's golf course. But all curling teams have one thing in common: they need sponsorship money to survive.

This has always been true, but with limited TV coverage, sponsorship often happened a little more silently pre-2000. Sometimes teams would have sponsor logos on their jackets, but more often than not, they relied on spreading the word of their sponsors in the newspaper or at events themselves or at various activation events. Once the Grand Slam of Curling permeated the airwaves in the early '00s, sponsors began to look at curlers differently: as walking billboards. It's tough to find an exact number for what a 30-second TV spot costs, but one thing is probably true: you could give a curling team what it costs to run one or two 30-second TV spots during the Grand Slam of Curling in exchange for them wearing your logo and having it visible, uninterrupted, for two hours. Curlers stand still a lot of the time, and having your logo readable on a curler is very easy. It's not on, say, a car going two hundred miles per hour, or on rink boards where the puck and players zip by constantly.

Companies have (mostly) figured this out, and now with the advent of "title sponsors" in curling and the advent of sublimation technology that allows logos to be printed directly on clothes and not ironed or sewn on, curling is in its NASCAR era. It is not uncommon to see a curling team's jacket with one main or "title" sponsor that takes up the front, and then a bunch of smaller sponsors occupying real estate on the sleeves, the back of the jacket, or a curler's pants. You want the entire jacket? You can pay for that too, and some companies have, making the entire jacket one big logo.

And you know what? It works. While I wish that companies didn't insist on most of the jackets being black or white so that their logos get maximum clarity, it does lend an air of professionalism to the sport, in a weird, capitalistic way. It shows that major companies are behind these curlers. It gives the jackets a design direction (because, let's face it, the old style of jacket that was basically some combination of geometric shapes looked terrible). And it's an indication that curling is moving toward being a sport these athletes can all do in a professional capacity, which can't be seen as a bad thing. Plus...

3. EVERYTHING FITS AND CURLERS LOOK LIKE ATHLETES

Era: 2010–present

As we have spent a lot of time discussing so far, curlers are not only athletes now, but also people who look like athletes. They have muscles. They have toned bodies. In short, curlers are hot. And look, some curlers were hot back in the day too, but the clothes did not match up, as jackets and pants were baggy, shoes were ugly, and everyone was smoking.

You don't have to go too far back into curling history—as we've noted above—to find that women's only options were skirts with nylons underneath or something resembling a wildly ill-fitting palazzo pant. Fortunately, it didn't take too long after yoga pants came along for curlers to figure out they could wear those on the ice too, and for the first time ever, female curlers began to dress like athletes. The idea that men could wear jackets that actually fit them and didn't simply droop off their shoulders like a beagle's ears was just as good. And the short-sleeved shirt that curlers began to prefer in size "schmeedium," which displayed biceps rippling as the curlers were sweeping, showed the world that curling was no longer the domain of beer bellies and bingo wings.

While I understand that athletic fashion in general has had a long way to go—seriously, look at how large the soccer jerseys of David Beckham were—athletes in other sports tended to wear clothes that fit, and it didn't take much to see an athlete in a sport on TV and understand they took care of their body and put effort into being strong. Curlers looked like they borrowed hand-me-downs from their older siblings' closet, in terms of both fit and style. I have this ranked so highly, even though it's not technically a specific "curling fashion," because I do think the simple idea of showcasing curlers as athletes and having their clothes reflect that has led to the surge in the sport's popularity, particularly during the Olympics. The sport has gained respect and a following because people are starting to see that no, they can't actually do what top-level curlers do, and the new fashion is a big part of it.

2. CARDIGANS

Era: 1960s–1990s

Now that I've spent the last two entries discussing how great the modern game is, and how we've really got the fashions dialled in, it's time to acknowledge that the best curling fashion overall, throughout the sport's entire history, is the cardigan. Yes, I know this is No. 2 on the list, but No. 1 is its own thing, and is specific to one team. So when we are talking about the best overall fashion choice, used by many teams over the years, we are talking about the humble, the beautiful, cardigan sweater.

First of all, it makes sense. Curling is now played mainly in hockey arenas, where the building temperature is regulated and doesn't affect the temperature of the ice. Most curlers want something lighter, and most curlers who sweep will play the entire game in a T-shirt. Back in the day, though, when most curling games were played in dank curling clubs on the Canadian Prairies that were heated by steam or coal or whatever they used to heat buildings in the '60s and '70s, and the walls were as thin as two-ply, curlers were cold. Even the sweepers. You could see your breath. You weren't exactly out on the pond, but you weren't far off. And so you needed something to play in that kept you warm. Something like a thick, wool, cable-knit cardigan. And not only were you warm, but damn, you looked good.

I'd implore you to spend a nice evening curled up by the fire while treating yourself to a Google search of "curling cardigans." You're gonna love what you see. Pinterest boards have nothing on how nice these things were. Shawl collars, chunky buttons, and, at the top levels, absolutely beautiful patches and stitchwork that showed who you were and who you were playing for. The Brier was riddled with gorgeously coloured handmade cardigans with intricate handmade patches. I'm getting misty just thinking about it. One thing the sublimated curling jackets of today don't allow is a ton of variety. Most are black or white, and almost all are made of the same material, and fit the same. It's a good look, but it's not a classic look. The cardigan is a classic look that has never gotten old, something that instantly and positively dates old curling clips, and something that really fits the kitschy, down-home nature of the sport.

Mix that in with a corn broom, a cigarette or a pipe, a tam, and some plaid pants? Now you've got a real look going. It is no longer practical at all to wear something like that, for the same reason that NHL teams never went back to wool sweaters after they figured out how to properly heat arenas. But I wish it were, because we are never getting it back again, and that was truly curling's golden era of fashion.

1. "THE PANTS"

Era: 2008–16

Surprisingly, curlers don't get asked about the sport too often. People don't really understand it, so they're afraid to ask, or they don't even understand that you're good at it.[1] They know that curling is something you "do," but they don't really understand the amount of time you're putting into it or how much it means to you. And look, maybe this is different for top teams, but I'm still imagining that even if you're Rachel Homan or Brad Gushue, you still do a lot of explaining about how good you are at the sport. It just comes with the territory. But then came "the Pants."

For a good two to four years, any time someone asked me about curling or mentioned the sport to me,

1 The number of times over the years that I have had to explain to people that my team was on the World rankings—yes we were in the top 25, yes, there are more than 25 teams in the curling world, but no, I wasn't a contender for the Olympics—is too many to count.

they referred to "the Pants." Now, it probably helped that "the Pants" got a ton of press at the 2010 Olympics, which were in Vancouver, where I lived at the time, but it was one of the only times that curling fully crossed over into the mainstream. Even today, 15 years after those Olympics, I still have people asking me about them. "Is that the sport where the guys wore those pants?" "Do you know the guys who wore the pants?" "What was the deal with the pants?"

The answers are yes, yes, and well, let me explain. Like a lot of the best things in life, there wasn't really a plan. It may shock you to learn that curlers don't all care about what they wear. In fact, most don't care at all, which does explain some of the same-y stuff you see out on the ice at various events. Most curling teams have a fashion person whose job it is to collaborate with their sponsors and the athletic wear company to design a jacket. The odd team, like Team Rachel Homan, has a graphic designer in-house, and so they do all their own designs.[2] Others work with a designer to come up with the right thing. And no one cares about the pants.

It was actually the curlers of earlier eras who were inventive with the pants, as they curled in slacks and so

2 Emma Miskew, a member of Team Homan, has a career as a designer, and has designed curling jackets not only for her own team, but for a host of others and some national championships.

had options. It was not unusual to see teams wearing houndstooth or gingham patterns out on the ice in varying "respectable" shades like grey, brown, khaki, and tan. At some point in the '80s and '90s, black became the couleur du jour, and very few curling teams strayed from that. You might get the odd grey or navy, but it was 95 per cent black. Black pants or black skirts, and that was it.

Enter Christoffer Svae.

Norway's outgoing second was helping to prepare his team for the 2010 Vancouver Olympics and was sent the wrong pants by a curling supplier. For the Olympics, most sporting associations will provide the jackets to fit with sponsor mandates and create a uniform look across events, but the pants aren't provided to curlers, as the associations also want the curlers to feel comfortable in whatever they'd normally curl in. Of course, for most teams, this means wearing a normal black curling pant, perhaps emblazoned with their country's flag or their curling association logo. When those showed up wrong, Svae had to hop into action.

He was scouring the internet for pants that might match Norway's colours: red, navy, and white. He found Loudmouth, a brand of golf pants that had become best known for sponsoring John Daly, perhaps golf's foremost loudmouth. The pants were argyle in pattern and the colours matched Norway's perfectly. Without telling his team, Svae ordered a set and hoped they'd work for the sport's showcase event, taking place for the first time as a non-demonstration Olympic sport in Canada, the country with what is easily the game's largest audience. In short, a lot of eyeballs were going to be on the curling. And a *lot* of eyeballs were going to be on Norway's pants.

At first, his teammates hated them. Torger Nergård, the third, and Thomas Ulsrud, the skip, were eight and nine years older than Svae. They had no doubt grown up in an era when flashiness was just not a part of the game, especially not at the Olympics. It would also be one thing if Norway was a flash in the pan, a team just happy to be at the Olympics and nothing more. But that couldn't have been further from the truth: they were one of the favourites, coming off back-to-back bronze medals at the World Championships. They were in the mix with Canada's Kevin Martin and Great Britain's David Murdoch. They couldn't show up wearing these pants. But options were limited, and after trying them in practice, the team agreed to wear them in Vancouver. They were a hit.

Fans loved them. A Facebook group dedicated to them reached over six hundred thousand followers in a matter of a week. News outlets everywhere started talking about them in such breathless tones that they became referred to simply as "the Pants." In an Olympics taking place in Canada, the Pants got talked about in the same breath as Shaun White's dominant win in the halfpipe and the Canadian men's hockey team on their run to gold. The normally staid sport of curling was getting attention, all because of a random online order by a Norwegian curler. The king of Norway attended the gold medal game, and the Pants became a huge story back home too.

The team grew to love them as well, wearing them for many years after those Olympics ended. Svae told the *New York Times* that wearing those pants almost took the pressure off the team because even if they weren't playing well, they could look at each other and think "Well, you're dressed like a clown" and break the tension. It also inspired them, in a roundabout way. As lead—and one of the sport's great characters—Håvard Vad Petersson would say, the Pants were great to win in. You win and the pants are cool, you're unique, and everyone loves it. If you lose, then you're not only the guy who lost, but you looked like a clown doing it. So they figured, hey, why not do some winning in them?

And win they did. They would go on to win the silver medal at the 2010 Games, losing the final to Kevin Martin. They would then win back-to-back European Championships in 2010 and 2011, and the Worlds in 2014. It may not have been directly because of the Pants, but we can't discount that possibility, and to this day, they remain the only sporting fashion in curling to have transcended the sport, fully deserving of No. 1 on this list.

DAVID RULES
LET'S GO DAVE!
EAT SWEEP
don is da bomb
JEFF
GOOOOOOO GEOFF
YAY DON
MICHAEL ROCKS
HOT MIKE
CURL GIRL
GO SCOTT
SLIDE, SCOTT, SLIDE!
MIKE

CHAPTER 13

ALL-TIME FIRST-NAME TEAM

Men

As a sport that has been predominantly played by Canadians (most of whom have come from the Prairie regions of the country), curling has a bit of an issue: a lot of people who have curled happen to have the same names. How serious you think that issue is may vary, but the fact is that one of the most spirited debates you can have in curling is "Who is the best curler of all time named Kevin?" And this can be stretched even further: What's the All-Time First-Name Team? That is to say, if you had to construct teams made up only of players with the same first name, who would be the best? The race is much tighter than you think. We now have players named Yusuke and Jayden and Kibo and Magnus, there was a simpler time when almost every male curler had one of ten first names, allowing us to create teams that would have had some unbelievable games against each other.

For this exercise, I tried to keep players in their most natural positions, and factored in those organic fits when deciding who the better team would be when it was very close, particularly at the top.

TIER IV: THE VIBES ARE OFF

Look, these are all good teams. But on every squad, there's just something that's a little bit off. We've submitted a vibe check to the Official Vibe Check Machine and lights are blinking and buzzers are going off.

THE SCOTTS

Skip: Scott McDonald (CAN)
Third: Scott Howard (CAN)
Second: Scott Pfeifer (CAN)
Lead: Scott Bailey (CAN)

A lot of the teams on this list will have a problem, and that problem is that their back end is very good, but their front end is a little weaker. This team has the opposite problem, and I will grudgingly admit as a lead that that's a pretty big problem. Scott Pfeifer and Scott Bailey are two of the best ever at their positions, but Scott McDonald and Scott Howard, while both being very nice players, are not. I don't love their chances.

THE MICHAELS

Skip: Mike McEwen (CAN)

Third: Mike Harris (CAN)

Second: Mike Hay (SCO)

Lead: Michael Goodfellow (SCO)

I want to like this team. Mike McEwen is one of the best curlers of this generation. Mike Harris has an Olympic silver medal. Hay and Goodfellow have 11 World Championship appearances between them (and one title). The problem is, the accomplishments just don't add up in the way you want them to. Mike McEwen has yet to win the big one, losing a Brier and Olympic Trials final. Mike Harris didn't do much outside of that Olympics appearance. Hay's World title was as a fifth, and he was arguably more successful as a coach. Plus, Mike Harris never really played third. I can't get there.

THE MARK/MARCS

Skip: Mark Dacey (CAN)

Third: Mark Nichols (CAN)

Second: Marc Kennedy (CAN)

Lead: Mark Fenner (USA)

Although the middle of the lineup here is as good as it gets, with three-time Olympian and gold medallist Marc Kennedy in the two-hole and fellow gold medallist Mark

Nichols at third, it's the bookends that cause us a problem. Dacey is a Brier champion but fell short at the Worlds, and Mark Fenner, while solid, has yet to find his way to a World Men's podium or an Olympics out of the US.

TIER III: A SPOT OF TROUBLE

These teams are getting better, but almost every case has at least one spot that's not filled by one of the best-ever players. That's how good these lists are about to get.

THE JEFF/GEOFFS

Skip: Jeff Stoughton (CAN)
Third: Jeff Ryan (CAN)
Second: Jeff Sharp (CAN)
Lead: Geoff Walker (CAN)

I don't even know if we are allowed to include Geoff Walker here, given his name's spelling. That's enough to shift the vibes. One of my favourite tweets ever, from @mtobey:

> Anybody here named Jeff?
> Jeff: Yes
> Geoff: Yeos

In any case, you've got one of the top 10 skips ever in Jeff Stoughton, you've got six-time Brier champion and

Olympic bronze medallist Geoff Walker in there, but the vibes... They're still off. Jeff Sharp went to the Brier four times but never made the playoffs, and Jeff Ryan won a Brier and World title, but I don't think of him as among history's best thirds. They're losing a lot of close games.

THE PETERS

Skip: Peter "Peja" Lindholm (SWE)
Third: Pete Fenson (USA)
Second: Peter Corner (CAN)
Lead: Peter Smith (SCO)

If you had to make a team where every curler was from a different country, this is your winner right here, and it isn't close. And not only that, your fifth, Peter de Cruz, is also from a different country (Switzerland). My only issue here is the third spot. Pete Fenson is a lifetime skip, and while he was a very good player for many years, on the world stage, he only has two bronzes: one at the 2006 Olympics in what was probably the softest Olympic field ever, and another at the 1993 Worlds. I think all the thirds from here on down outplay him, and that's an issue. That said, they may play spoiler, given who'll be at skip.[1]

---

1 Peja Lindholm, in addition to being one of the best curlers ever, at one point had a winning streak against Kevin Martin that extended to 10 games. Most curlers have never beaten Kevin Martin 10 times

THE RICHARDS

Skip: Rick Folk (CAN)

Third: Richard Hart (CAN)

Second: Rick Lang (CAN)

Lead: Rick Sawatsky (CAN)

This team has a similar problem to the Peters', except their trouble spot is at lead and not at third, so that bumps them up one. Rick Sawatsky is a fine player, losing an Olympic Trials and Brier final and making the Brier 10 times. But he's likely not a hall of famer, and that holds this team back ever so slightly. Rich Hart also has an Olympic silver but only one Brier and world championship, and that will hold him back when compared with the thirds we are about to see.

TIER II: IT'S COMPLICATED

THE PATS

Skip: Pat Ryan (CAN)

Third: Pat Simmons (CAN)

Second: Patrick Hürlimann (SUI)

Lead: Pat Perroud (CAN)

---

total (or quite frankly, even once), never mind in a row. They could play spoiler. We'll see Kevin Martin on this list soon.

Is this team better than the Richards? Well, it's complicated. Pat Ryan has a very similar record to Rick Folk's, with three Briers and two world championships. Pat Simmons and Richard Hart are very close as well: one extra Brier for Simmons, but no Worlds or Olympic medal. It's the front end where this team diverges, as our only Olympic gold medallist on the team is Patrick Hürlimann, and we've got him down at second. Maybe he plays third over Simmons, I'll let you decide. And then Pat Perroud is the rare lead who's won two world championships playing for two different skips: Al Hackner in 1985 and Ed Werenich in 1990. He's the glue that will help this team come together.

THE DONS

Skip: Don Duguid (CAN)
Third: Don Walchuk (CAN)
Second: Don McKenzie (CAN)
Lead: Don Bartlett (CAN)

I love that this team is not the Donalds, but the Dons. How Canadian. This is also the only team where the bulk of these guys have actually played together, with Don Walchuk and Don McKenzie winning the silver medal at the 1985 Brier playing for Pat Ryan, with Don Bartlett as the alternate. Don Duguid won three Briers, including two consecutively in 1970 and 1971, and went on to be a beloved commentator of the sport for CBC. There's a lot to love here, and my complicated feelings about them probably have a lot to do with the fact that most of their success came before I was alive or watched a lot of curling. Maybe they're better than this ranking, I don't know. It's hard, okay?

THE JO(H)NS

Skip: John Shuster (USA)
Third: John Morris (CAN)
Second: Jon Mead (CAN)
Lead: John Landsteiner (USA)

This is painful to do. My name is John. I both have to leave myself off this team, and leave them out of the top three. I hate to do it. Every keystroke is like stabbing my fingertips with a tiny knife. But we have no choice. Although we do have arguably the best third of all time and a two-time Olympic gold medallist on the team in John Morris, and we have two other Olympic gold medallists in Johns Shuster and Landsteiner, we simply cannot say this team is better than those coming in the top three. Jon Mead is also a two-time Brier champ and a world champion to boot. It's just that John Shuster does not have the resumé as a skip to push this team into the top three. He's the US's most accomplished player ever, but unfortunately the US is not the curling power some other countries are.

I was also tempted to push this team into the top three. You know how we often joke that in Olympic hockey, Canada could send a B team and still have a chance to win gold? Well, that's the same here. The B team would feature John Epping at skip, John Ferguson at third, John Kawaja at second, and then any number of world champs to play lead: John Bryden, John Pearson. Look at that, I didn't even sneak myself onto the alt squad; at least you now know how objective I've been in the rest of the book. The point is, the Johns are mighty, and it's tough not to rank them higher up. But alas...

TIER I: THE TOP THREE

THE BRADS

Skip: Brad Gushue (CAN)
Third: Brad Jacobs (CAN)
Second: Brad Thiessen (CAN)
Lead: Brad Heidt (CAN)

I love this team. I love it because it has a skip who is in the GOAT conversation, with an Olympic gold medallist skip at third and a Brier champion at second, and also because it has Brier finalist skip Brad Heidt at lead. Anyone who knows Brad Heidt knows that this is an extremely funny choice. He's essentially only skipped, and qualifies as one of curling's ultimate characters. Combined with the fiery

Brad Jacobs, the caustic Brad Gushue, and the muted Brad Thiessen desperately trying to hold it all together, this will easily be the most fun team to watch. They're in the top three but could easily lose every game and finish at the bottom of the tournament. They could also easily win it. Grab your popcorn.

THE KEVINS

Skip: Kevin Martin (CAN)
Third: Kevin Koe (CAN)
Second: Kevin Park (CAN)
Lead: Kevin Marsh (CAN)

This team does not have the accomplishments, on paper, that the Pats or the Brads or the Johns do. But what they do have is Kevin Martin and Kevin Koe playing back end, which has some degree of inevitability to it. Like I said, this list is a vibe, and it's hard to imagine a team with those two at the back end not being the best. If you're talking about the best skip ever to play, it's Brad Gushue, it's Niklas Edin, and then it's the two Kevins. Having them on the same team feels like two supernovas colliding. No curling fan would be able to look away.

Plus, we have the bonus of Kevin Koe's experience in playing third earlier in his career, as he did for John Morris and then on his own team with Blake MacDonald, before he took over throwing last for good in 2009. In his day, people would describe Kevin Park as the best hitter on the planet, so bumping him from third to second is no issue. He also brings four Brier medals to the table, and a World silver. You might say that Kevin Marsh presents some of the same issues that Rick Sawatsky does, but he just lost the Brier final in 2024. He's getting better all the time, and here he has Kevin Martin as his skip and Kevin Koe as his third. That said, this team still just doesn't *quite* have enough. At some point, on-paper success matters. And the No. 1 team has it.

THE DAVIDS

Skip: David Murdoch (SCO)
Fourth: David Nedohin (CAN)
Second: David Hay (SCO)
Lead: David Smith (SCO)

Sure, this team doesn't have an Olympic gold medal. But it does have a silver. And eight world championships. *And* a whopping 27 World Championship appearances. Throw in some European titles on top of that, and David Nedohin's place on one of the greatest teams of all time, and you're cooking with gas. Plus, David Murdoch was a guy who proved he could beat Kevin Martin in the big games. Can they dismantle the Kevins? I'm not sure, but at some point, all the accolades have to count for something, and so I'm going to give the very, very slight nod to the Davids. Who knew the top first-name team would be mostly made up of Scots? I suppose they did invent the game, after all—with all the ingenuity that they didn't waste on thinking up given names for baby boys.

CHAPTER 14

ALL-TIME FIRST-NAME TEAM

Women

Or girls. It would appear that giving our kids the same 10 names hasn't only been a male issue. This exercise can easily apply to women's curling as well, and I'd argue there are some even more natural team fits here than there are on the men's side. Not only that, but our top team here is *dominant*. One name to rule them all.

TIER IV: THE KAITLYNS

Skip: Kaitlyn Lawes (CAN)

Third: Kaitlyn Jones (CAN)

Second: ???

Lead: ???

Okay, the Kaitlyns need two spares from the spare pool, but we have two women with probably the fourth or fifth most-popular way to spell Katelyn/Caitlin/Caitlyn/Kaitlyn/Cait-Lynn/Kaytlynne/K8lynn who have a wild number of accomplishments between them: World Juniors, World Women's, two Olympic golds. It's impressive, all things considered. Maybe a parent or two were inspired by all of Lawes's and Jones's winning and if we wait 20 years or so, we'll have some teammates who can join them.

TIER III: "WE NEED AN ELITE BACK-END PLAYER"

THE SELENA/SELINAS

Skip: Selena Njegovan (CAN)
Third: Selina Gafner (SUI)
Second: Selina Witschonke (SUI)
Lead: Selina Rychiger (SUI)

Two of these three Selinas currently play on the same team, and all three Selinas are from Switzerland. The chemistry is built-in. We'd have Selina Witschonke hold the broom while Selena Njegovan is throwing, because Gafner and Rychiger are among the top five sweeping pairs currently in the women's game. Njegovan has mostly played third but does have skipping bona fides, playing skip for Tracy Fleury and Kaitlyn Lawes when they've been out, and with some success. You add in World Junior titles for Rychiger/Gafner and two World silvers for Witschonke, to go along with two European titles, and you've got a great squad, though one that lacks a star skip. Plus, "the Selena/Selinas" sounds like a girl-pop group, and I love that for them.

THE SARA(H)S

Skip: Sara McManus (SWE)
Third: Sarah Wilkes (CAN)
Second: Sara Carlsson (SWE)
Lead: Sarah Potts (CAN)

Sara McManus played skip for only a brief time in juniors, so despite her fantastic resumé that includes an Olympic gold medal, this team lives on this tier as it has a ton of great players but no natural skip. Sarah Wilkes did win a Scotties playing third, but she's transformed into one of the best leads in the world now, winning two World titles with Team Homan at that position. Sara Carlsson has a World title as a second, but didn't accomplish much past that, and Sarah Potts has yet to win the big one. Lots to like, but lacking the true quality to push them over the top.

THE ANN(E)S

Skip: Anne Merklinger (CAN)
Third: Anne Jøtun (NOR)
Second: Anne Laird (SCO)
Lead: Ann Swisshelm (USA)

This team solves the problem the Sara(h)s have, in that it has an elite skip in four-time Scotties medallist (and one-time champ) Anne Merklinger, but then the rest of the team is leads. In fact, it was hard to even decide who would play third and second, because all three have never really played anything else, but I decided to go with the two-time world champ Jøtun. Now, we could cheat and put Kim Eun-jung on the team, since her English name is "Annie," but that does feel a bit unfair. This team does, however, remind me of the Peters from the men's chapter, in that if we had to put a team together where we could use no more than one player from a given country, it may come out on top.

THE KATES

Skip: Kate Cameron (CAN)
Third: Ekaterina "Russian Kate" Galkina (RUS)
Second: Kate Goodhelpsen (CAN)
Lead: Kate Horne (CAN)

Kate Cameron has skipped the last few years after a long while playing third, and has looked good doing it, winning a Scotties bronze in 2024. Kate Goodhelpsen has a World Junior title. Kate Horne has a World silver and a Scotties title to go along with six Scotties appearances. And yes, we do call Ekaterina Galkina "Russian Kate," and no, it isn't weird. She's been to the Worlds 10 times, with two bronzes, and has World Junior, World University, and European Championships medals in her curling bag. Unfortunately, all of those came from playing second, and Kate Cameron doesn't have the resumé that some of the other skips on this list have, so this team sits nearer the bottom.

TIER II: THE ELITE

THE AL(L)ISONS

Skip: Alison Goring (CAN)
Third: Allison Pottinger (USA)
Second: Ali Kreviazuk (CAN)
Lead: Alli Flaxey (CAN)

This is where it starts to get really good. Elite players up and down the lineup. Did you know Allison Pottinger has been to the Worlds 13 times? I did not. Incredible. Plus, she's got a World title to go along with Goring's 1990 World bronze and Kreviazuk's World silver and bronzes. Alli Flaxey has been a career back-end player, but it's been proven lots of times that thirds can move down to lead easier than skips or seconds can, so we love having her there with her recent Roar of the Rings appearance. Plus, this team has a built-in theme song, sung by Elvis Costello. Doesn't get any better than that.

THE KELL(E)YS

Skip: Kelley Law (CAN)

Third: Kelly Scott (CAN)

Second: Kelly Schafer (née Wood) (SCO)

Lead: Kelly Middaugh (CAN)

Being from British Columbia, the two Kell(e)ys (Law and Scott) were my world growing up. I remember getting to meet and curl with Kelley Law shortly after she went to the 2002 Olympics and I thought it was the greatest thing that could've ever happened to 17-year-old me. Hell, I'm 39 years old now and it still might be. We've got an Olympic bronze here to go along with several World titles, a boatload of Scotties appearances, and we have this: the greatest curling love story ever told.

While Kelly Schafer (then Wood) was representing Scotland at the 2010 World Championships in Swift Current, Saskatchewan, she met the mayor, Jerrod Schafer, and a romance developed. She ended up moving to Swift Current, where they later got married. *She went to the Worlds and began an international romance with the mayor.* It's a true Canadian love story. Someone get Netflix on the phone.

THE HEATHERS

Skip: Heather Houston (CAN)

Third: Heather Nedohin (CAN)

Second: Heather Smith (CAN)

Lead: Heather Strong (CAN)

Originally, I had the Heathers in the top three. Let's face it, the credentials are there. Four Scotties titles. One World title, and four Worlds medals. *Twenty-eight* Scotties appearances. It's an incredible team resumé. Unfortunately, the team I have in third has the Greatest of All Time, and sometimes you just can't compete with that. And although Heather Strong went to 12 Scotties, she never medalled. Plus, this team is plagued with the "all skips" syndrome, the opposite of how we classify a really good album. So it's tough to know if Heather Smith would be good at second or Strong good at lead, and it's tough to decide whether Heather Houston or Heather Nedohin should skip, so while the team I have just edging them out for the top three may not have the titles these ladies do, they just *feel* like they are a stronger team. Sorry, Heathers, but you do have the consolation of the best team promo opportunity: the poster for the 1988 film *Heathers*, with just a slight Photoshop job. Actually, maybe someone reading this can do that for me and send it to me. Thank you.

TIER I: THE TOP THREE

THE JENNIFERS

Skip: Jennifer Jones (CAN)

Third: Jenn Hanna (CAN)

Second: Jennifer Dodds (SCO)

Lead: Jenn Baxter (CAN)

When you have the GOAT at skip, anything is possible, but this team just can't be any higher, owing to the lack of elite credentials elsewhere in the lineup. But Jennifer Jones is almost a team resumé on her own. Her record is, quite frankly, insane, and you can't stare at it too long for fear of being blinded by the light glaring off the trophies. Eighteen Scotties appearances (out of arguably the hardest province, Manitoba). Six titles. Four World medals, including two golds. Olympic gold medallist (leading the first and only team to do it undefeated). Throw in a Canadian Junior title. Hell, the Order of Manitoba. Jenn Jones is an island, her own country in the world of curling. Her gravitational pull ensures the Jenns get to the top three. Well, that and Jenn Dodds winning a surprise Olympic gold medal in 2022, when her team, skipped by Eve Muirhead, battled their way through a stacked field. Dodds is also an accomplished mixed doubles player, having won a World title with Bruce Mouat in 2021 and a World silver, again with Bruce, in 2025. Unfortunately, the accomplishments of Jenns Hanna and Baxter can't match up. Jenn Hanna had the undesirable honour of having the best seat in the house to watch one of the best shots of all time, as she lost the 2005 Scotties to her first-name teammate Jennifer Jones, in that shot we discussed in Chapter 7. Hanna returned to the Scotties only once after that, while Jenn Baxter has been to seven Scotties but has only found the podium once. They're good, they got the GOAT, but they just don't quite match up to our top two.

THE CATHYS

Skip: Cathy King (CAN)
Third: Cathy Overton-Clapham (CAN)
Second: Cathy Gauthier (CAN)
Lead: Cathy Shaw (CAN)

Two things I adore about this team:

1. "Cathy" feels like a very Canadian name, and I'm very here for it.
2. I love that it's all "Cathy." There are no Kathys here, or Cathies, or Kathies, or even Catherines. It's Team Cathy, baby, and that's the way it is.

The big question here is "Can Cathy Shaw play lead?" but I'll go ahead and say that with her resumé of two

Canadian Junior titles and five Scotties appearances, including a gold and a silver, she can. She also won the Scotties in the final year before there even was a World Women's Curling Championship, but let's assume she wins a World medal there (Canada medalled at 20 of the first 21 Women's Worlds, so it feels like a safe assumption). Then we have the venerable Cathy King at skip, with her seven Scotties appearances (out of Alberta, one of the toughest provinces to win), her one Scotties title, her World Senior title, and her cache of Tour wins. Cathy Gauthier has only been to four Scotties, but she won three of them (insane record). She's also got two World medals, and her son is a World Junior champ (I don't know if that counts for anything). And then, if Jennifer Jones is an island, Cathy O is the islet right next door. (Or maybe they'd prefer the islands to be on opposite sides of the world. That's okay too). Thirteen Scotties appearances at both skip and third (out of arguably the hardest province, as she's also a Manitoban). Five Scotties titles (and 10 overall medals). Three World medals. Ten Grand Slam victories. Hell, at age 48 she came one win away from going to the Olympics.

This team? It's good. Really good. Oh, and my third favourite thing? Their bench would have Cathy Walter (formerly Caudle) and Cathy Cunningham on it, who have 17 Scotties appearances, one championship, and two other medals between them. Go on, girls.

THE ANNAS

Skip: Anna Hasselborg (SWE)

Third: Anna Sidorova (RUS)

Second: Anna Sloan (SCO)

Lead: Anna Le Moine (SWE)

We've decided since the turn of the century that Olympic medals and appearances mean more than anything else in this sport, and this is the only team on this entire list that has multiple players who have even *played* in the Olympics, never mind having multiple gold medals. Hell, Anna Le Moine herself has more Olympic gold medals than any other team on this list (aside from the Kaitlyns but... they only have two players). Add in Anna

Hasselborg's 2018 gold and Anna Sloan's 2014 bronze and you've got a team that has one heck of an Olympic medal collection (not to mention Hasselborg's bronze in 2022). Every player on the team has also appeared in at least one Olympic Games, and they have seven appearances in total among them. And that's not all.

Twenty-five World Championship appearances. Three gold medals. Thirteen total medals. I won't even bother counting the European Championships appearances and medals, because there's a ton. You'd lose count. Thirteen Grand Slam victories too. It's honestly absurd. No team even comes close, and we also have most of the players in their natural positions. Anna Sloan was always a great hitter, so it doesn't seem like a stretch to find her at second, and Sidorova shouldn't have any issue ceding the skipping reins to Hasselborg and making a great vice. And Anna Le Moine, almost poetically for the purposes of this exercise, played lead her entire career. This team is a juggernaut. On the men's side, it's pretty easy to imagine that if we played some sort of tournament with those teams, any one of the top five or six could win. But this tournament isn't a contest, it's a bloodbath. The Annas win, and they win handily.

Who knew that the All-Time Men's First-Name Team would only have one Canadian on it, and the Women's would have zero? We've gotta start banding together to name our kids the same thing or we're gonna keep losing our grip on curling dominance, even more than we already have.

And wait!

Mixed doubles is a fairly new discipline and does not have enough history to merit its own chapter yet, but that said, it's the Kerri/Kerrys: Kerri Einarson, she of four Scotties titles, and Kerry Burtnyk, with two Brier titles and a world championship. Plus, they live about an hour apart in Manitoba and would be able to practice together a lot. And if Kerri Einarson gets hurt, we've got Kerry Galusha and her 21 Scotties appearances to step right in. Although the Jamies (with Sinclair and Koe) and the Kell(e)ys (with Law or Scott and Kelly Knapp) get close, it's all the Kerri/Kerrys.

CHAPTER 15

BROOMGATE

May I break the fourth wall a little bit? Is there a fourth wall in books? Maybe not. The fourth page? I don't know. I just feel like it's only appropriate to begin this chapter with some inside information. I first started pitching this book four years ago (never give up!), and when you pitch a book, you often give a list of the things you intend to write about. Here's one of the ideas I suggested:

> Roughly four years ago, there was a huge scandal that rocked curling, which we dubbed "#Broomgate," as broom manufacturers figured out a way to utilize a fabric so powerful that the game of curling became the easiest thing on earth. That sounds like a made-up sentence, but I promise it's true, and it sent the game scrambling for an entire year. I tell the story of that here.

As you may be aware, these three sentences became the basis for the most successful curling podcast of all time: *Broomgate: A Curling Scandal* (always be pitching!). I think we can all agree, that worked out best for everybody, as the audio medium is better suited to that story than having me ramble on about it here. If you haven't listened to it, I think it would be nice if you did. I'm very proud of it. And this chapter is going to be all about it. You will still be able to enjoy this chapter without listening to it, but you might like the chapter more if you have.

On Episode 6 of the podcast, my showrunner, Kathleen Goldhar, sat down with me and asked me some questions about the show and our process, and I joked that there was a different version of the podcast for curlers. Something like *Broomgate: Curler's Version.* The original intention of *Broomgate* was always to attract a mainstream audience to care about curling. In fact, throughout my entire "curling media career," that's all I've ever wanted to do. I love the sport, and I want other people to care about it. In relation to the podcast, that meant leaving some things on the cutting room floor that would have been interesting only to curlers, and given that those tapes are almost certainly never going to see the light of day, I thought it might be fun to explore some of those things here. Although I'm not necessarily going to blow the lid off everything, here are some of the most interesting things that got left out of the podcast, and other assorted notes about our sport's biggest scandal.

Just before we get there, a quick refresher for those of you who listened to *Broomgate* and can't remember all the salient details, or for those who didn't listen at all. Of course, I'd prefer you took a three-hour break from this book to listen to it, but hey, I understand. Time is valuable.

Broomgate was a scandal involving, as we have mentioned and as the name suggests, brooms. A new manufacturer came on the scene in the late 2000s/early 2010s called Hardline, and with them came a new broom: the icePad. It was mostly used at the club level for a few years, and then I started using it. (I was sort of a key player in the whole thing—I get into it on the podcast.) After I used it, I convinced a top curler named Mike McEwen to use it. He and his team went on to have one of the greatest curling seasons of all time, in 2014–15, making the final in nearly every event they played in, and winning most of them. They made almost double the amount of money that second place did on the money list, and became the World No. 1.

This caught the attention of some curlers in the 2015 off-season, as they were surprised, maybe not by Mike's success (he was very good before the brooms too), but by just *how* successful he was. An off-season training camp led Brad Gushue, one of the world's other top curlers, to discover that these brooms, if used by only one sweeper at a time, could have an immense effect on the rock. They were pretty much the most powerful brooms anyone had ever seen. He debuted this new method at the start of the 2015–16 season, and everything went pear-shaped.

Curlers started to investigate Mike's previous season and his success, and wondered how much the brooms were a part of it. The camaraderie and social fabric of the game broke down as curlers fought with each other to figure out a way forward for the sport. The podcast looks at all of that conflict, plus the eventual solution, which was to change the broom's fabric. More on that below.

I think you're all caught up. So let's crash the 'gate.

1. THE SCOTTIES, THE BRIER, AND THE WORLDS WERE A MESS

One of the main things I got asked by curlers in the wake of *Broomgate* is why we didn't talk about the three biggest tournaments on the curling calendar in any given year: the men's and women's Canadian championships and the Worlds. The Sweeping Summit world conference was in May, after the curling season ended. Which meant we had to get through these tournaments without exact rules in place. We did ask the curlers about it, but we felt that the incident at Toronto's High Park (a dispute between curlers that is described in detail in the *Broomgate* podcast) was the flashpoint of the whole mess, and was a somewhat similar story to the big three championships (curlers mad, rules confusing, everyone unhappy). Here are some fun facts for you:

ALL THE CHAMPIONSHIPS HAD SOME FORM OF ADJUSTED RULES.

While we didn't know everything there was to know about what the brooms could do and which brooms were good or bad to use, we did feel confident in trying to put some rules in place for the major tournaments. It started with the Scotties, where hair brooms were banned for use by anyone other than a skip or vice using it in the house. This rule would end up holding up for the Brier and Worlds. Before that, the "directional fabric" had been banned—i.e., the Hardline icePad—but really all that meant was Hardline teams had to ditch the plastic insert that went between the foam and the fabric, and they had to use a newly approved fabric developed by Hardline that ended up being just as good (or close enough) to their previous one. And as we would learn at the Sweeping Summit, banning just the icePad was a pretty funny decision, given that the curlers figured out that literally every commercially available head at the time could direct the stones: the BalancePlus EQ, the Goldline Norway, and so on. This solved some problems, but not the ones presented by teams still being able to use foam-and-fabric brooms that could direct the stones.

THERE WAS AN ATTEMPTED "GENTLEMEN'S AGREEMENT" BEFORE THE BRIER.

We discuss gentlemen's agreements quite a bit in the pod, because before Broomgate (the scandal, not the podcast; you'll know the difference when I use italics), there wasn't a ton of dedicated rules for sweeping or, well, anything. And this was mainly because the curlers usually found a way to sort it out among themselves, whether through a brief discussion before a tournament, over beers in the curling club lounge, or with pre-tournament phone calls and emails. Curlers are doing a similar thing now with "Foamgate," transpiring as I write this (more on that later), and it's amusing to know that it was attempted in the Broomgate year too.

Ben Hebert sent an email to the teams before the Brier, because one of the issues they had attempted to address at the Scotties was teams switching brooms mid-game: one thing some savvy teams had realized was that a skip—who barely swept in the course of the game—could keep a fresh head for the entire game, and then a teammate could switch brooms with them whenever they needed a really sharp head for a key shot. Ben, who described that action as "bush league" in the email, was hoping to create an agreement among teams that they wouldn't do that, and some teams suggested in reply that they could convince Curling Canada to set up a sticker system, so that the teams would be sure that the sweepers never switched brooms. Curling Canada did not do that, and not all the teams agreed to abide by the gentleman's agreement.

Playing with Kevin Koe at the time, Ben and his fellow front-ender Brent Laing decided they were going to master these brooms. If you can't beat 'em, or whatever. They would switch their brooms around so the thrower was almost always using the same broom. That kept that one broom sharp, and then they would only use it for down-weight takeouts, and wouldn't sweep the whole time—just a "tickle," they called it. They were able to control down-weight shots better than anyone, and by managing to keep one broom head "fresh" for most of the game, out of the three they had access to, they were able to manipulate rocks in a way no other team could. They won. Then they went to the Worlds. *The Worlds had no gentleman's agreement and even more lax rules.*

Once again, at the rules meeting before the Worlds started, Ben and Team Koe tried to get World Curling to understand what had just happened at the Brier. They recommended curlers be prevented from switching brooms among themselves, and that everyone be forced to have a single broom throughout the game. World Curling went in a different direction. Not only did they condone switching, but they allowed the team to have a designated "throwing broom" in addition to one broom per team member. Some teams have skips or other team members who use a broom they like as a "throwing broom," and it's usually old. Something they prefer the head shape of, or the feel of. Team Koe didn't have that issue. So they designated one of their regular brooms as the "throwing broom," and then had four brooms in their hands. At the Brier, they were able to keep one broom as fresh as possible for certain finesse shots. Now they could keep two like that. It was an advantage that their opposition found insurmountable. Team Koe won the Worlds.

And if anyone was wondering, the effect of the brooms was obvious in the rest of the men's World standings as well. Rasmus Stjerne from Denmark lost the final to Kevin Koe. Before that, he was last at the Worlds in 2014 and last at the 2014 European Championships, where he went 1–8 and got Denmark relegated to the European B division. He went from the 2015 European B Championships to the 2016 World silver medal.[1] John

1 If you finish within a certain number of teams at the bottom of the Euros, your team is relegated to the Euro Bs, and you have to win your way back to the top division of the Europeans, which awards places at the World Championships, which I guess are technically the "Euro As," but no one calls them that. Making the World final

Shuster of the United States won the bronze, and though he did win the 2018 Olympic gold medal, that remains his best-ever finish at a Worlds. Yusuke Morozumi from Japan came fourth. He made the Worlds five other times, and never even made the playoffs, never mind a medal game. The brooms made a huge difference for the teams who had figured out how to use them. Perhaps even more telling? Niklas Edin, who, as Brad Gushue made a point of telling me, never quite figured out how to use the brooms, missed the playoffs that year. He's won the damn thing seven times. Go figure.

2. THE STORY OF "OFF THE SHELF" BROOMS

One of the slapdash rules that were made in the midst of the Broomgate season, but that didn't get a lot of airtime, was that players had to use brooms that were "commercially available," meaning they had to be available for purchase by anyone, and not just given to or made available to top players. The rule wasn't given a ton of attention by the general public at the time, because that

---

in the same year you come out of the Euro Bs has never happened before or since. It's also lucky the Worlds that year were in Europe, granting Switzerland a host berth. Had the Worlds been in Canada, Denmark wouldn't have even been invited, as they were given the last spot by virtue of their European B win.

wasn't something the general public knew about. But it was something the players absolutely wanted. Why?

Well, the answer is obvious, isn't it? In a climate where there are virtually no rules about which brooms a team can use, teams would have their manufacturers experiment with different things, whether fabric materials, handles, head shapes, or otherwise, in an attempt to gain an advantage. Hell, Curling Canada came right out and said before the 2010 Olympics that they were developing a broom that would only be available for use by the Canadian teams at that year's Olympics. Everyone in the curling world just shrugged and said, "Yeah, okay." The Canadian teams didn't end up using that broom (which would go on to be licensed by BalancePlus and become known as their "Equalizer" or "EQ" head) because it was a bit too powerful and they couldn't figure out how best to weaponize it. We were five years away from the one-sweeper method, so it is what it is.

When Mike McEwen and Reid Carruthers began using the icePad, and then people started to ask questions about it after Brad Gushue exposed the brooms in the 2015 season, a lot of curlers' minds went to, "Well, Mike and Reid helped Hardline develop a broomhead just for them." This was unequivocally not true, and both of those teams—as well as any other Hardline team at the time, like the one I was on—was using the icePads that were available in pro shops across the country. But because teams in the past *had* asked their manufacturers to make things just for them and no one else, they assumed that had to be what was happening here. It was a fun little wrinkle that I really couldn't get enough people to speak with me about on the record, so we had to leave it out of the podcast, but it was at least somewhat ironic that some of the teams that were so mad about brooms in the Broomgate year were actively using items that no one else could use because they understood the value of a more powerful broom.

Another fun wrinkle to this? The Goldline website fiasco. Most players, by the turn of the calendar to 2016, had figured out that hair brooms were as good or better than the fabric alternatives, but they hadn't been fully banned yet. As we headed into provincial playdown season, teams were being allowed to use hair brooms in their championships that would determine the Brier and Scotties representatives. By that time, teams had also been able to experiment with hair brooms enough that they had figured out Goldline offered the most effective model. Once teams were aware they could use hair brooms at their playdowns, they rushed to buy them so that they didn't get left in the dust by their competitors who were using them. So the Goldline hair heads eventually sold out. Maybe you see where I'm going with this.

This all came to a head at the Alberta Scotties, where a team in the final was using those Goldline hair heads, but because those hair heads were sold out, Goldline had removed the product from their website. As we know, the rules stipulated that heads had to be "commercially available," and with the product disappearing from the website, some teams began to argue that those Goldline hair heads were therefore illegal. This led the teams who were using them to frantically phone Goldline to get the product put back on the website, but with a "Sold Out" sticker, so that it could be seen as technically commercially available, but with the caveat that Goldline had run out. It all led to a very contentious Alberta final in which Chelsea Carey won—she would go on to win the Scotties outright—with some of the most vicious post-game interviews we have ever seen. What a silly and insane time for the sport.

3. THE JAMES BOND–IAN NATURE OF THE EARLY SCIENCE

One of the people I was most excited to talk to for the podcast was Graham Prouse. He was a member of World Curling's board in the Broomgate year, and the VP of World Curling when we spoke to him for the podcast. World Curling had never really gone on the record about their thoughts on Broomgate at that time. Graham ended up spearheading a small committee to deal with the Broomgate issues. Why? Well, because he lived in Canada.

One part of the story we didn't really cover is how most of the issues in the Broomgate year happened in Canada and affected mostly Canadian teams. Of course, there was the handful of international teams at the time who regularly played in Slams, but the Slam field wasn't as international then as it is now—it was a small handful. Many of the European and Asian teams didn't think much about Broomgate because very few of their teams were using Hardline then, and they weren't competing much in Canada, where Brad Gushue's one-sweeper method was being adopted by teams left and right.

Graham was partnered with Hugh Millikin, a Canadian expat who had moved to Australia and represented them at the World Championships 11 times throughout the '90s and '00s. Hugh was also working for World Curling at the time, and the winds of Broomgate were beginning to blow across curling when World Curling had their first championships of the year, the Pacific-Asia Championships in Almaty, Kazakhstan, in November. Remember, the High Park incident happened about six weeks earlier, in October. That was the real flashpoint of the whole thing. A rival broom company to Hardline, BalancePlus, had developed a head that was like the icePad on steroids, which they called "Black Magic." It was so effective that it was quite literally taking chunks out of the pebble on the ice surface. This forced an emergency "meeting" (a very heated one) in the middle of the event to try to quell the arms race brewing among the top teams.

World Curling had put a moratorium on the original Hardline icePads at those Pacific-Asia Championships, but it wasn't an issue, because none of the teams there were using them. But World Curling knew the Worlds would be coming soon enough, and Curling Canada was looking for direction for their provincial Scotties and Brier playdowns, which were less than two months away. Curlers were getting into heated arguments at Slams, fighting with each other, and World Curling knew it was their duty to try to prevent that from happening. Even worse, the European Championships were coming up in a week, starting just six days after the Pacific-Asia Championships, and teams in the European Championships were planning to use those brooms. World Curling was worried they wouldn't be able to extend the moratorium to the Europeans without any scientific evidence to back it.

And so, in the thick of the night, Hugh Millikin flew to Uppsala, Sweden, a town of roughly 175,000 about an hour north of Stockholm. Why Uppsala? The university there had been studying the effects of brushes on curling ice, and had started that study a couple of years earlier. Graham Prouse was among the World Curling officials who recognized that the rule book needed more on sweeping and equipment in general, and so they were working toward that, but then found out all at once that they were far too late. Uppsala had some research, but nothing with the newer brooms, and so after placing some calls, Hugh Millikin was able to secure a 36-hour window in which to fly from Kazakhstan to Uppsala, use the brooms there, get some scientific evidence, and then fly home to Australia, where he had work commitments.

After arriving in Uppsala in the dead of night, Hugh was able to head out in the morning with the research team there. Their technology included dental cement, which they used to take impressions of the ice surface after the brooms were used. Then they could look at those impressions through a very high-powered electron microscope. With this process, they were able to see exactly what the brooms were doing to the ice. Using not only the Hardline icePad but also a number of commercially available brooms, they found the smoking gun.

Graham was waiting impatiently at his home in British Columbia for word from Hugh Millikin that the brooms were too powerful, so they could extend the moratorium to the European Championships. At 2 a.m. BC time, just days before the start of the Europeans, Hugh was able to send photos of the research in Uppsala to Graham that confirmed what they had thought: the brooms were causing small scratches in the ice. And as you may remember from the podcast, one of the only rules in curling at the time about sweeping was that you could not knowingly damage the ice with your broom. Armed with these photos, World Curling was able to extend the moratorium to the Europeans and onward into the rest of the competitive season.

The only problem? All they could confirm for sure was that the Hardline icePad's plastic insert, which went between the foam and the fabric, was causing a real issue. They needed to do much more testing to be able to move on to banning anything else, even though they felt they had quite a bit of evidence from the session in Uppsala that many of the commercially available brooms at the time were a problem.

And that's how we ended up with the Scotties, Brier, and Worlds being a mess. Still, a very cool story, and one where I prefer to imagine Mr. Millikin absconding from Uppsala in a black car with a briefcase handcuffed to his wrist, photo evidence from the electron microscope inside. Swept, not stirred.

4. THE SCIENCE OF IT ALL

I would've loved to dig more into the science itself. I think our production team wisely identified and agreed early on that going deep on the actual science of curling, from why rocks curl to what brooms do, and from how ice conditions affect play to what *these* brooms specifically did, would've been boring as hell to a lot of listeners.

But I'm not a lot of listeners. And the reality is that one of the main reasons Broomgate happened in the first place is that there is still so much we don't know about the physics of curling. Most other sports we have pretty much drilled down at this point. If your hockey stick or golf club has a more flexible shaft, it will give you more of a "whip" effect when you lean on it. Baseball pitchers now hire coaches that specialize in things like generating spin rate, improving pitches with various arm angles, and preserving arm health. The list goes on. In curling, we are pretty new at this. We've come a long way from some Scottish lads in the 16th century deciding to slide rocks along a pond's surface.

It's hard to generate rules for a sport and its equipment when, as a whole, you really have no idea what that equipment is doing. As we say in the podcast, we always knew that sweeping could make rocks move straighter and go farther. But even on that, we didn't know exactly the best ways to do that, other than to just sweep. We lacked knowledge about who should be the inside sweeper; we always swept with two people; we thought hair brooms were only for really frosty conditions; and more. It's cringey to watch old highlights of huge shots where the sweepers are doing it all wrong, given what we know now. And what we know now still isn't everything! But you gain some sympathy for World Curling for not having rules in the rule book about sweeping when, if you asked most curlers what sweeping could do, they only thought two things, and nothing else.

So it would've been a lot of fun to dive really deep on the science that came out of the studies in the Broomgate year: hearing what Uppsala University had to say about those tests they did with Hugh Millikin; learning what Eugene Hritzuk and his team at the University of Saskatchewan are currently discovering in their study, which is now almost five years in. And an overlooked detail: although we mentioned in the podcast that the Canadian National Research Council was involved in the Sweeping Summit, we didn't mention that Megan Balsdon, a fantastic curler herself who has made both the Canadian Junior and Scotties championships, was on that research team.

Megan, who is a PhD candidate with a master's in biomechanical engineering, is someone I would've loved to sit down with and absolutely nerd out. I feel 100 per cent positive that I wouldn't know even 20 per cent of what she was talking about, considering that the last science class I took was Biology 11 in high school, where I finished with a whopping 78 per cent grade, but it would've been cool to hear exactly how the testing worked at the Sweeping Summit and what she believes about the physics of it all. Maybe I'll just do that podcast anyway, and it can be me and her sitting down for the science nerds. I'll need something to do after this book is finished anyway.

And it doesn't necessarily need its own section, but we interviewed Ben Hebert, and I wish we could've just aired that entire thing. Because he is one of the best talkers in the game and also one of the most honest, Ben's interview for the podcast was phenomenal, but because he was not involved in the incident at High Park—his team was curling across the country in Edmonton at the time, where a mini–High Park was taking place at the Crestwood Curling Club–it didn't make sense to have him as one of the podcast's main characters. Rest assured, he was great.

As I said in Episode 6, I would've loved to make *Broomgate* 10 or 15 or 20 episodes long and just let everyone cook, but I think ultimately we settled in the right place. With the success of the pod, people have asked me about what's next. What's the next big curling scandal to talk about? Well, there haven't been any nearly as huge as Broomgate, or at least none with as catchy a title. But there have been some curling incidents, from small to big, and maybe there's something there.

CHAPTER 16

CURLING'S OTHER #GATES

Well, this is my promise to you: this is a mini-chapter. In curling, we have had some arguments. Some scandals. But nothing came close to Broomgate. So here is a quick summary of curling's other #gates, whether they were big enough to be worthy of a hashtag or not.

#FOAMGATE

Some are calling this Broomgate 2.0, and it's happening right now, as I write this book. So there isn't a definitive answer here, but it stands to reason that if curlers felt in the Broomgate year that the broomhead fabric had to be changed, and the other piece of a broomhead is foam, then eventually we'd tamper with the foam enough that *it* needed to be changed too.

World Curling changed the standards for "how hard is too hard" (get your mind out of the gutter) when it

THE WALL SWEEP JOURNAL
SCANDAL!
FOAM SWEET FOAM
ASKING THE HARD QUESTIONS
A SLICE OF SASS
Paul Gowsell orders a pizza to the ice
WINNING BY A HAIR (BROOM)
Martin vs. Howard
ROCKS & ROIDS:
YES, CURLERS DO GET TESTED (REALLY)
WHO RUNS THE WORLD? CURLS.
JEN GATES SUES CANADIAN AUTHOR FOR "BRINGING ME INTO THIS"
ICE, ICE MAYBE
SCOTS TAKE THE HEAT

comes to foam, and so manufacturers started to push their foam right up to the brink. (The harder the foam, the more pressure you can exert on the ice surface; the more pressure you can exert, the greater the effect you can have on the ice and, therefore, the stone.) Some curlers didn't like that. They thought it was too hard, and that foams were starting to get effective to the point that rock manipulation began to resemble the Broomgate year. By the time this book is published, there may already be a solution and we'll be moved on to the next obvious scandal with curling equipment: #HandleGate.

#PIZZAGATE

No, this is not related to that QAnon thing during the 2016 election. Curling had its own Pizzagate *way* before that—OMG trendsetters!—and it's also very, very different.

Paul Gowsell was one of curling's legendary characters, a brash young man from Calgary who showed up on the scene in the late '70s and treated curling like a true sport in a way that no one had before, with regards to trying to get in his opponents' heads.

As we've established, curling is a big proponent of everyone playing nice in the sandbox, but Gowsell was all too happy to kick over your sandcastle and then tell you it was your fault. Gowsell kept long hair and a beard and always wore plaid pants, causing Hec Gervais, a rival skip, to famously say that if Gowsell shaved his face and got two haircuts, then maybe he'd be all right.

Gowsell was playing at a bonspiel in Regina and, upset with his opponents' slow play, ordered a pizza to be delivered to the ice. He then ate it while his opponent brooded over shots.

Gowsell would later claim it was simply because the line was too long for food at the curling club in between the semis and final, but I've played in enough tournaments to know that in those situations, curlers get to skip the line. Urban legend later told people Gowsell actually beat his opponent when their rock picked (changed course) after hitting an olive from the pizza. That's how deep the lore with Gowsell went, and if social media had existed in the '70s, #Pizzagate would've been real, and *much* cooler than what it became. Seriously. Don't look it up now.

#REPLAYGATE

It was the 2009 Roar of the Rings—the Canadian Olympic Trials—and it was the final round-robin game between Kevin Martin and Glenn Howard. The winner would get a bye straight to the final, and the loser would have to go through the semi. In the ninth end, Kevin Martin had the hammer and was drawing to lie two. His draw was a little bit heavy, and Ben Hebert lifted his hair broom in front of the rock, which is a no-no. Curling brooms must finish away from the rock, so that no debris is purposely left in the path of the travelling stone.

As soon as the rock comes to rest, Glenn Howard's third, Rich Hart, gets upset with Ben, noting that Ben went "straight up in the air with a hair broom." Hair brooms tend to pick up more debris, which is why Hart feels that is notable. Ben denies this claim, and Rich tells him to watch the replay on the scoreboard at Rexall Place in Edmonton. TSN obliges, and the whole arena watches as Ben does what Rich said he did. It doesn't appear that the rock picked, so in the grand scheme of things, it doesn't matter, but it has the curling world atwitter because direct confrontations between athletes on the ice like this happen so seldomly. Martin goes on to win that game and win the final, also against Team Howard.

#ICEGATE

As we have established, curling ice is a lot different from the ice for other sports. It is manicured and highly controlled, and needs the right environment to be made correctly. As you might imagine, ice-making technology has improved by leaps and bounds over the last 50 years, as we've begun to move big curling tournaments into larger arenas, and we've learned more about the science and technique behind proper ice-making. That hasn't stopped some tournaments from having legendarily bad ice.

The Brier tournaments of 1973 and 1979 both got nicknamed "the Bad Ice Brier," for different reasons. In 1973, the icemakers had trouble taming the Klondike Gardens in Edmonton,[1] leading to a strange combination of very heavy frost on some parts of the ice and small pools of water in other spots. In 1979, the Brier was held at the Ottawa Civic Centre, a real building that does still exist and that you can find evidence of on the internet, but organizers borrowed the rocks from the local curling club, and they were terrible. Mismatched, pitted, and dead, the rocks were so bad that players actually held a vote halfway through the Brier to see if they'd like to switch. Bad rocks are worse for drawing teams than hitting ones, and so the hitting teams outnumbered the draw teams and kept them. Curling Canada now has its

1 An arena so bad it doesn't have a Wikipedia entry, nor is it even searchable on Google. I truly don't even know what it is. Sounds cool, though.

own set of rocks it uses at national championships to avoid such an issue.

And perhaps the granddaddy of them all,[2] the 2005 Women's Worlds. We talked about Jennifer Jones's amazing shot to win her first-ever Scotties in 2005—simply one of the best curling shots ever, and a coming-out party for a skip who had been knocking on the door for a long time. Her reward? Getting to play at the most cursed Worlds of all time.

Held at the Lagoon Leisure Centre in Paisley, Scotland (already a bad sign that *lagoon* is in the name), the tournament was plagued by horrendous ice. Sitting next door to an aquatics centre—as in, literally sharing a wall with a pool—the ice was impossible to maintain. A big part of making curling ice is controlling the humidity in the building, and as you might imagine, doing that next to an indoor, heated swimming pool is very difficult. The organizing committee also refused to pay for deionized water, a big part of curling pebble. The ice was so bad that they had to postpone the fourth draw of the tournament, and finally relented and agreed to pay for deionized water. That didn't help.

2 Usually, this term is used positively. I don't know if you can use it negatively or not. Let's try it out.

In addition to the ice being horrible, there were no time clocks. Typically, time clocks at major events are run by volunteers. The folks in Scotland wished to be paid, and World Curling wouldn't pay them. World Curling's solution? To let an official arbitrarily decide to remove rocks if they felt a team was playing too slowly. This has never been done in curling before or since, and it cost the Russians a game. It was a disaster. Jennifer Jones finished out of the medals, but Anette Norberg, one of the sport's greats, persevered through the horrible conditions to win.

#SUBSTANCEGATE

People are always surprised to learn that in the history of curling as an Olympic sport, athletes have tested positive for banned substances. "Why bother?" they say. "What could possibly be the advantage?" Well, you can see today's curling athletes for yourself now and probably figure it out. Everyone is strong, and needs to be strong. If you can't sweep, you can't play. Certain steroids also allow your body to recover more quickly after an aerobic event. Because so much of curling is a dramatic aerobic event, followed by a quick bout of recovery, followed by another aerobic event, there is a potential benefit to taking a substance that could allow your body to recover more quickly and thereby offer you an advantage in a game situation.

Weirdly enough, the first person to be suspended for the use of a banned substance was actually an alternate player. Matt Dumontelle, serving as fifth for Brad Jacobs at the 2013 Worlds, tested positive after the final (Jacobs lost), and received a two-year ban. Now, taking steroids while acting as the fifth player is something I can definitely get behind as a "why bother?" situation.

Then a Russian player, Alexander Krushelnitskiy, tested positive for meldonium after the 2018 Olympics in South Korea. Meldonium was the substance that so many Russian athletes were caught using at the 2014 Olympics in Sochi that the Russian athletes in Pyeongchang had to compete under the "Olympic Athletes of Russia" banner. Having won the bronze medal in mixed doubles, Krushelnitskiy was forced to surrender the medal to their opposition from Norway after the positive test. Even more juicy? Krushelnitskiy's defence was that he was poisoned by a Russian curling teammate who was envious that Krushelnitskiy had been selected for the Olympics instead of him, spiking Krushelnitskiy's drink with meldonium at a training camp. This defence was not accepted by the IOC, and Krushelnitskiy was banned for four years.

And perhaps the most high-profile case just concluded in the early days of 2025, after Briane Harris,

Winnipeg native and member of Team Kerri Einarson, was suspended on the eve of the 2024 Scotties for testing positive for a banned substance, Ligandrol. The anti-doping laws are so strict that Harris was not only banished from competition, but also forced not to practice or to enter any curling facility during her ban. She also couldn't contact her teammates. She appealed the decision, saying her husband had unknowingly ingested the substance through a supplement and then passed it to her during intimate contact. After a year of fighting, Harris won her appeal and was reinstated, but it was a drama that gripped the curling world for both its rarity and its severity.

#JENGATES

Jen Gates is a curler who has been to the Scotties four times, winning a silver as an alternate player for Krista McCarville in 2022. She also won two Canadian university titles. No scandal, just a last name that fits the chapter.

I could've also used her sister, #AmandaGates, to execute the same joke. Amanda has also been to the Scotties four times. Successful curling family!

Of course, a sport that has existed for this long could have many other scandals, big and small, to discuss. There's probably a bunch I don't even know about.

The point is, we love a petty squabble in our little, insular sport, and I'm sure we'll enjoy many more in the years to come.

CHAPTER 17

BUILDING THE PERFECT CURLER

Frankenstein. The Modern Prometheus. As one of literature's most vile and memorable creations, Mary Shelley's cobbled-together monster has dominated Halloween costume racks and children's nightmares for generations. The weird part is, the monster in the book (named "Frankenstein's Monster" and not "Frankenstein," as Frankenstein is the doctor, as any pedant at a party will tell you) isn't intended to be all that scary. The monster actually longs to be a part of humanity, asking the doctor to make him a female companion, and saving a child from drowning. It's humanity who ends up making him a monster.

Anyway, all of that is to say that I'm imagining a similar scenario here: what if I created the dream curler using parts of some of the best curlers of all time? That curler would no doubt be scary, but curling is a friendly sport. I'm going to tap into some of Frankenstein's

Monster's gentle nature and create what I think would be the best curler ever. And I will be honest: if this was a real person, they would look insanely messed up. But hey, so did the Monster.

Hair: BALD. Let's start from the top. And look, most of the other body parts will come from specific curlers, but given the perhaps sensitive nature of this topic, I won't single out any one curler here. But if you look at the history of men's curling, especially in Canada, a great number of the best curlers ever have been bald. The European curlers have managed to find success while hanging on to their hair, as have Niklas Edin and Bruce Mouat and Peja Lindholm and Thomas Ulsrud; but in Canada, if you wanna be the guy, you gotta be bald.

Eyes: Rachel Homan. No one in curling history has had a steelier gaze, to the point that for years we didn't even know Rachel had an amazing sense of humour because we were all at least a little bit scared by how she looks when she's delivering a stone. This is never more evident than when she is throwing a takeout. She is looking at the rocks down at the other end like she is going to pulverize them just with her eyes. And then, of course, it also helps to be one of the greatest of all time, because she usually does. Pulverize them, I mean.

Glasses: Marie-France Larouche. Call it the revenge of the rainbow safety strap. There have been many bespectacled curlers throughout the game's history, on account of us being massive nerds, but perhaps no one made them more iconic that Québec's beloved daughter, MFL. Playing at 11 Scotties and finishing on the podium twice, with a World Mixed and a Canadian Juniors also on her resumé, Marie-France was a staple for any curling fan whose formative years in the game were the late '90s to late '00s, i.e., me. She wore a similar style of frame for that entire decade, very narrow over the eyes, with varying degrees of thickness, and they always looked cool.

Ears/Brain: Jennifer Jones. As someone who has interviewed curlers for over a decade and has often chased weird facts about players to stump them, I think my favourite fact that I know about a curler is that Jennifer Jones has supersonic hearing. A few curlers told me about it over the years, and then, when I started working with her husband Brent Laing, doing commentary for the Grand Slam of Curling, he confirmed it for me. He said she can not only hear things from a great distance, but also track several conversations at once, which, as he jokingly mentioned, may not be an ideal trait in a significant other.

And what's between the ears? A brain. There have been few finer strategists over the years than Jones, who, for my money, is one of the absolute best late-game players there is. She has managed to win more games that a team would normally lose based on a late-game scoreboard than anyone. It's probably all the tremendous listening she did over the years that helped her hone her game and made her the GOAT.

Mouth: Ben Hebert. If you know anything about curling, this one is pretty self-explanatory. A curler so funny and so outrageous that Sportsnet gave him his own show—appropriately titled *The Sheet Show*—Ben is the only choice here. But it isn't just jokes and fun stuff that tumble out of Ben's mouth on the regular; he is also known as one of the best teammates of all time, playing for a handful of the top teams in curling for his entire career as a lead. He's also been known to contribute more to team strategy discussions than most leads, because he thinks the game so well and is a great leader. Also, I have to say that he is a beast on the broom and will probably be mad I didn't select his arms, but here we are.

Arms: Joanne Courtney. Who else could it be? Almost single-handedly revolutionizing sweeping in the women's game, Joanne dedicated herself to being the best sweeper and was routinely at the top of every "best sweeper" list, even if the rest of the list was men. It helped her to win a

Canadian Mixed Doubles title; it got her on the best team in the world at the time (Team Homan). And it wasn't a surprise that when her full-time curling career ended, she just decided to do some triathlons for fun. Those arms had to do something!

Hands: Rick Folk. We do need to tap into the legends of the game somewhere on our Curling Monster, and there's no better way to do it than to have the steady hands of one of the greats, Rick Folk. We know he shook a lot of hands in his career as a politician, but it's not the pre- and post-game ritual we're after here. The two-time world champion had already done most of his winning by the time I got into the sport, but I'm not sure any skip made more shots with their hands than Rick did. Known for preferring a quieter weight on takeouts than most, and for being able to draw to basically any spot on the sheet, Rick didn't have what you'd call a "textbook" delivery. The broom was often just a suggestion for Rick, and not a target. But the way he was able to use his hands to get the stone to where he wanted it to go, almost two hundred feet away, is unparalleled in the game, and we need them releasing all of the Monster's stones.

Legs: Amos Mosaner. The more we learn about sweeping, the more we discover that while it certainly does help to be strong and fit, it also helps a lot to be tall. The leverage that you can create on the broom by being tall and the angles it allows for you to attack the sweep make a huge difference. You can still be a good sweeper if you're short, so don't despair, but if you can find a way to be tall, do that. And Amos is among the tallest players ever to be this good at the game. Standing 6′5″, Amos is a great thrower and great sweeper, and his height helped him win the 2022 Olympic mixed doubles gold medal, defying the odds. Can't have height without long legs (well, it's tough), and Amos is giving them to our monster.

Calves: I would be remiss if I didn't mention the man who has the self-proclaimed "best legs in curling," Matt Dunstone. Although "the Sheriff" may have incredible calves, he is also a little bit on the short side, and we want our Curling Monster to be able to do it all. So let's take Amos's long tree-trunks and snap Matty D's calves on there like Lego pieces. We are working now.

Feet: Matt Hamilton. I grew up in an era when the "customized curling shoe" had only just begun, and for many years, we were never quite able to master it. Curlers would get skate shoes done up with sliders on the bottom, because skate shoes often had flat soles, making it easier for the shoemaker to get the slider on there properly.[1] As shoemakers got better at affixing sliders to shoes and we got better at having taste, Matt Hamilton took advantage of this perhaps better than anyone, bringing out a whole line of very expensive and very nice shoes to curl in. I'm not sure if he was the first to curl in Jordans, but he certainly made it look the best. I also felt like I had to include him here because, in reality, we probably should have his hair too, as it is long and majestic, but we went with bald excellence instead.

Aura: Alina Pätz. Yes, yes, I know that "aura" is also not a body part, but I think anyone who read *Frankenstein* knows that aura was a fairly important part of understanding why Frankenstein's Monster met with the fate that he did. In my case, though, aura is positive, and I have never heard a curler be called "cool" more in my life than the Swiss last-rock thrower Alina Pätz. She's won six World Championships, which you can't do without being cool under pressure. But it's more than that with Alina: she just looks cool on the ice. I don't like to use the word *swagger*, but it's probably the best way to describe how she carries herself on the ice. Professional curlers want to

1 I think in curling we probably call them shoemakers and not cobblers? I don't know. Curlbblers? No, I don't think it's that.

play with her, amateur curlers want to be her. Sometimes the coolest people just have that certain something you can't describe, and Alina has that in spades.

And here are some other little, fun parts I'd take:

Russ Howard's scream: Especially once it got to Wednesday or Thursday of a week-long event. Have you ever heard a dying moose? Me neither, but I bet it sounds something close to Russ losing his mind while calling line on a takeout in the second end of a game.

Marc Kennedy's side part: One of the few curlers whose status-as-an-elite-player-to-baldness ratio is the highest (or lowest?), and except for a brief "ski jump" phase that we all had, Marc's had an absolutely perfect side part and doesn't look like his hairline has receded an inch. Envious!

Pooks and Fergie's dance moves: Rachelle Brown and Dana Ferguson (known collectively as "Pooks and Fergie") became known for dancing in the most high-pressure situations, and it endeared them to curling fans worldwide, including me. Plus, they danced their way to a Scotties title, which no one has really done before.

Eve Muirhead's accent: If we're building our ideal curler, we can't have it speaking with a Canadian hoser accent, as much as that might be fitting. No, we're going to go with Eve's Scottish brogue, as pleasant to listen to as the bagpipes she can also play (and yes, bagpipes are pleasant to listen to, and yes, we also get her bagpipe-playing ability as part of this Frankencurler).

Kevin Koe's big shot: There are many debates about the GOAT (in fact, we are about to have one right here in this very book), and Kevin Koe is included in that conversation, though probably isn't the GOAT. But that's okay, because I think a lot of curlers, if given the choice of one person to throw the one big shot to win the game, would pick Kevin Koe. I can't think of a shot type he hasn't made to win, from drawing the pin in pressure situations like Brier and Olympic Trials finals to the big hero shot doubles and angle runs to get the job done.

Kelly Scott's encouragement: Never has there been a skip in history who was nicer to her team after they missed than Kelly Scott. No one has said the words "Good try" and actually meant them more than Kelly Scott. As a forever lead, I can't actually fathom how good that must have felt. Probably really good.

Sherry Anderson's longevity: Curling is a life-long sport, as any good curler will tell you when they're trying to encourage you to play the game. Lots of curlers have been good at it for a very long time, but there's something about Sherry Anderson going to her first Scotties in 1994, when she was 30, and playing her last one in 2021, when she was 57, that stands out to me. Not to mention that she became eligible for Seniors (50-plus) in 2014 and then made the final in 2016, and then won the Canadian Seniors five times in a row (a record), from 2017 to 2022. She also won three World Seniors in that time. Most curlers dream of being able to keep up at that level for that long.

Reid Carruthers's timeouts: Reid is a fantastic curler, of course, but I can't get enough of watching his timeout style as coach of Team Einarson. He marches down the ice, immediately presents the options with confidence, and lets the team decide. You can tell he is a teacher. As a bonus, he will have a cool toque on while he's doing this.

Lisa Weagle's ticks: If we're having Kevin Koe's big shot, then we gotta show some leads love and have Lisa Weagle's ticks, as she became the first lead to truly master the shot, previously thought to be very difficult. Helping Team Homan dominate a style they essentially invented—and subsequently crushed other teams with—Lisa's mastery of that one shot was so complete that people started calling the tick "the Weagle," which might be curling's only mononymous shot. Slay.

Thomas Ulsrud's calendar picture: Although he was in the curling calendar several times, you know the picture I'm talking about. The curling world lost a giant when Ulsrud passed away from cancer in 2022, a great man with a great talent for the game. But we also lost one of our most handsome guys ever. That 2014 calendar pic is insane. It should be illegal to look that good and that jacked when you're 43.

CHAPTER 18

WHO IS THE GREATEST MALE CURLER OF ALL TIME?

I was trying to avoid talking about this. It's a debate that rages on, from the accounts with 23 followers on social media to every curling club lounge around the world. Even some of the elite curlers themselves wade into the debate, usually stumping for someone else, but sometimes, even for themselves. Who is the GOAT?

It's a debate so contentious that curlers do feel the need to speak on their own behalf, as though this was a political race and not just a fun thing to debate among curling fans. I think that's partly why I didn't necessarily want to discuss it. There have been many great curlers over the years. Who you think is the GOAT probably depends a lot on how old you are. It's like the old chestnut that your favourite *Saturday Night Live* cast is probably the one that was around when you were a teenager and therefore found *SNL* funnier than you would later in life. It's probably the same with the curling GOAT.

The foundational players of your early days of curling, your first idols, are perhaps the ones that stick with you the most.

And what about position? Is the GOAT necessarily a skip? A lot of people might tell you that third is actually the more challenging position to play. You have to sweep, for starters. But you also have to balance the energy between the skip and the rest of the team, you have to have *every* shot in your tool kit, and you have to have the ability to bail out your front end if they don't set up the end well before your skip goes to throw. Also using this logic, is the GOAT necessarily one player? Or should we think of the GOAT as more of a Greatest Team of All Time discussion, and not just a single player?

For each gender group we have a clear top three in the conversation. And then, yes, I will decide at the end of each summary who the GOATs are. It will not be easy. But I am resilient, I am tough, and I am ready for the inevitable swath of opinions that I will receive online now that this book is out in the world. Here we go!

THE NARROW MISSES

It's always hard to stack non-Canadian teams up against Canadian ones in these debates (which we will get to in more detail), because international teams do not have the gauntlet of the Brier with which to draw even more comparisons with their peers. Would international teams have as much success at the Worlds if they had to make it through an arguably tougher tournament to get there? Do they even get there as many times? Or at all? It makes it hard. But with that said, some international curlers in the discussion would include:

David Murdoch, Scotland: Olympic silver, two World titles, three European titles, two World Junior titles

Thomas Ulsrud, Norway: Olympic silver, one World title, two European titles

Peja Lindholm, Sweden: three World titles, two European titles, one World Junior title

And the closest...

Bruce Mouat, Scotland: Olympic silver, two World titles, four European titles, one World Mixed Doubles title, one World Junior title, one World University title.

Bruce is carving a path in this sport that at the young age of 30 has him potentially destined for the GOAT crown. He's won everything there is to win outside of an Olympic gold medal already (which he may have done in 2026, depending on when you're reading this book). He already has 10 Slam victories and looks well on his way to becoming the all-time leader there (not to mention that he became the first skip ever to win four in the same season, this past year). And he has done all this in the sport's hardest era. It's only his age and the fact his career isn't as close to completion as others on the list that keep him from being in GOAT contention, but as far as raw talent goes, he may be the best we have ever seen.

Beside them are a few of the international Olympic gold medal winners, like Patrick Hürlimann of Switzerland, Pål Trulsen of Norway, and John Shuster of the United States, though none of them won a World title, so they cannot be the GOAT. On to the Canadians:

Ernie Richardson: This is a classic example of a guy who might be your GOAT if you're reading this book and you're older than 70. Winning four Briers in five years with a team composed of his brothers, Richardson also won all four of those World Championships, and topped most GOAT lists until the 1990s rolled around.

Randy Ferbey: Another four-time Worlds winner, Ferbey also won the Brier six times, a record he held for almost 20 years but now shares with another guy that's coming up on this list. Ferbey had longevity, winning his first Brier in 1988 and his last 17 years later, in 2005, and his "Ferbey Four" rink is one of the most iconic in history. However, there are a couple of potential detractions here: no Olympic success, and those four Brier wins with the

Ferbey Four took place in Brier fields that were diminished owing to teams boycotting the Brier in favour of the Grand Slams.

Kevin Koe: Yet another four-time winner, Kevin Koe has won a quartet of Briers, but managed World gold only twice. And while he did win an Olympic Trials, the team missed the podium at the 2018 Olympics in Pyeongchang, the first and only Canadian men's team to do so since curling was introduced to the Olympics as a full sport in 1998. As I said earlier, he might be the best pure "big shot" shooter in the game's history, but the resumé is not quite there.

Russ Howard: Although he only managed to win the Brier twice, in 1987 and 1993, Russ went to 14 Briers, and when he retired from the game in 2009, he had been to more Briers and played in more Brier games than anyone else (that record has since been broken and Russ now sits 10th all-time). He also parachuted onto Team Gushue in 2005 just in time to help them to a surprise win at the Olympic Trials and an Olympic gold. The entirety of his career just doesn't stack up to some others, though.

Glenn Howard: Russ's brother Glenn is the toughest one to leave off of the list. He went to 20 Briers out of one of the most consistently tough provinces to win, Ontario. Of those 20 Briers, he was on the podium 14 times, winning four times. And each of those four World Championship appearances resulted in a gold medal, with two of those wins 25 years apart, his first in 1987 and his last in 2012. He has also played on two of the most iconic teams of all-time, with his brother Russ, Wayne Middaugh, and Peter Corner, and then later with himself at skip, Richard Hart at third, and Brent Laing and Craig Savill rounding out the list. He has 16 Grand Slam titles too. Unfortunately, the lack of Olympic success leaves him just on the outside when it comes to GOAT talk. But it's so close.

And now, it is time to head to the official Court of Curling to decide who is, once and for all, the GOAT of men's curling. We have our best lawyers at the ready, a judge who looks both regal and stern as judges are wont to do, and a jury. Well, the jury is me. Much easier than 12 people, I think.

THE TOP THREE

BRAD GUSHUE

Olympics: one gold medal (2006), one bronze (2022)

Brier: six wins (2017, 2018, 2020, 2022, 2023, 2024)

Worlds: one win (2017), four silvers (2018, 2022, 2023, 2024)

Grand Slam of Curling titles: 15

Best team: 2014–22: Mark Nichols (third), Brett Gallant (second), Geoff Walker (lead)

The evidence: Weirdly, when TSN did their "Canada's All-Time Greatest Men's Curlers" list not so long ago, in 2019, Brad Gushue ranked ninth. Since then, all he's done is add four more Briers to his trophy case, three more World silvers, and a trip to the Olympics, where he won bronze. He has the most games played at the Brier, and the most wins. He has the coveted Olympic gold medal that, at this point in curling history, probably any GOAT contender would need to have, and he also has multiple Olympic appearances out of Canada, something only a handful of curlers in this country have ever done, and only one other skip (Kevin Martin). He has also been so good over the last decade that he has forced all the other Canadian teams to consolidate their power to play against him, something that news outlets have dubbed "the Gushue Effect." He also has 15 Grand Slam titles, which is third among skips, but Kevin Martin and Glenn Howard both won the bulk of theirs in a less competitive era, so you could make the case that he is the best Grand Slams player ever as well. And the icing on the cake: he has also won a Canadian Mixed Doubles title with Kerri Einarson and two World Junior titles, once as an alternate and once as a skip.

The prosecution: If we were to imagine this as a courtroom drama, and we were prosecuting the case *against* Brad Gushue being the GOAT, there are a few factors.

The first are those pesky Brier records. Brad Gushue has spent his entire curling life living in St. John's, Newfoundland. This is commendable, because I'm not sure if you've ever flown into or out of St. John's, but it isn't easy. To go almost anywhere west of Ontario, you have to take a connecting flight. Hell, even some places in the Maritimes, directly south of St. John's, demand you fly west to Montreal first. He's dedicated a lot of his life to unnecessary travel, the unavailability of ice, and a dearth of solid teammates, just to keep his life on the Rock. Although that is impressive, it's also fair to say that he may not have been to the Brier 22 times if he hadn't had much easier competition, compared with his rivals', to win his province and get to the Brier. If we're applying that argument to international teams who don't have to win the Brier to get to the Worlds, then we probably have to apply it to a team that didn't have to come through the Manitoba, Alberta, or Ontario gauntlet just to appear at the Brier.

Not only that, but it took Brad 14 years and 13 tries to win his first one. There is some degree of "Well, if you play in the Brier long enough and you're a good enough team, eventually you'll win" at play. And then there is also the matter of the World titles. The other skips on this list have more, and in one case, many more. Although he has made the final in every Worlds he's been in, you can make the case that only one Worlds is not enough to be considered the GOAT.

The defence: The Brier thing gets debunked fairly quickly when you consider that although he did take 14 years to win his first one, he went on to win six of the next seven, and has won more than any other skip. Fifty years from now, we will barely be discussing the fact that it took him so long to win his first, and we'll just be busy counting the trophies in his case. As for the Worlds, you can also justify his record by saying that he's played in a more competitive international era than any skip before him. Although the Brier has always been a tremendously difficult tournament to win, it was long known that the Worlds always offered a few "free spaces on the bingo card" to the Canadian winner. In fact, Canadians who won the Brier won the Worlds so often that it was an expectation to win, not unlike Team Canada playing at hockey events. That is no longer the case. It is likely harder now to win the Worlds than it is to win the Brier (or at the very least, as hard), with the carrot of the Olympic gold medal convincing sport and curling federations around the globe to invest more money in curling than they ever had before. The fact that Gushue has made the final in all five of his World appearances is actually a fact worth celebrating, and not denigrating.

KEVIN MARTIN

Olympics: one gold medal (2010), one silver (2002)

Brier: four wins (1991, 1997, 2008, 2009)

Worlds: one win (2008), two silvers (1991, 2009)

Grand Slam of Curling titles: 18

Best team: 2006–13: John Morris (third), Marc Kennedy (second), Ben Hebert (lead)

The evidence: Most lists that have been made in the last decade regarding the men's GOAT have Kevin Martin at the top, and it's for good reason. Kevin has not only the resumé, with two Olympic medals and a World title, but also a few unique distinctions. The first is his longevity. He made it to the Olympics when it was a demonstration sport in 1992, and then made it again 18 years later in 2010 (and won). He also had a ton of success with three different teams, which is something Brad Gushue hasn't really done. Almost all of Brad Gushue's success has come with Mark Nichols at third at the shakiest of times, and Geoff Walker and Brett Gallant at the best. Kevin won the Brier with three completely different players in 1991, 1997, and 2008–09, and his two Olympic medals also came with completely different rosters. Aside from that, off the ice Kevin is perhaps the most influential figure in the history of the game, leading teams into the professionalism era by treating the sport and his team more like a business than anyone else, and by being one of the instrumental figures in the creation of the Grand Slam of Curling, eschewing several years of Brier competition to do so.

The prosecution: The first and most glaring fact that anyone will point to here is the number of World titles. He has only one win and only two silvers, easily the emptiest of any trophy case among the men in consideration for GOAT. If curling had never become an Olympic sport, we may not have Kevin in any sort of GOAT discussion because of his lack of World titles. Another fact that people often point to when discussing Kevin as the GOAT is his standing atop the podium of Grand Slam–winning skips, officially having won 18 of them, all as a skip. There are a few issues you could poke at with that record: first of all, three of those Players' Championship wins were before the Grand Slam of Curling was even founded. Yes, the Players' Championship was turned into an official GSOC event (and still exists today), but it wasn't a Grand Slam event then. Second, even if you subtract those three, 12 of his 15 Slam wins came in 2010 or before, when the Slams were not nearly as competitive as they are today. In contrast, all but one of Brad Gushue's 15 wins have come after 2010, with four of them coming in the last five years, when the Slams have been at their most competitive and toughest to win.

The defence: The fear factor. I've been around curling for almost 30 years now, and I have never seen a team that had the aura that the 2006–13 Kevin Martin team did. As I said, we used to joke that teams would pay the "Kevin Martin tax," which was the name for what would happen when a team that was outside the top 10 played Kevin and surrendered a big end to him early because they started doing things *they wouldn't normally do*, because they felt like they had to pull out extra stops to beat him. I can't count the number of times I was in the same bonspiel as Team Martin, and I'd look over and they'd scored 3 or 4 in the first end. And if they got a lead, they were nigh unbeatable, especially in the days of the four-rock free guard zone. They were so good at hitting that you just couldn't find your way back against them. And overall results? They have those too. If you combine their records at the 2008 and 2009 Brier and Worlds and the 2010 Olympics, they went 60–5. They were undefeated in both Briers, undefeated at the Olympics (still the only men's winner to do so), and won four of those five championships. It's as good a three-year run as any team has had.

Does your GOAT need to include stuff in the builder category? I've seen it used in other sports and your mileage may vary, but I'd argue Kevin has had a greater impact on the game off the ice than any of the other candidates for the GOAT. He helped establish the Grand

Slams (and was willing to sacrifice some of his prime to do it) and has done a lot for the television product as both a player and a broadcaster. And if and when curling becomes a truly professional sport, one where the world's best curlers can afford to concentrate on no professional endeavour other than the game, it will be very hard to argue that he was not one of the first people — if not *the* first person—to really try to get it there.

And no, curling is not yet a professional sport. Most curlers have a day job. The ones who don't are getting by on a combination of their winnings and their sponsorship money, but in most cases, that's not as much as you could make if you had a "regular" day job, or it only lasts for the short window in which you are on top of the game. In 2026, the Curling Group is introducing Rock League, the first professional sports league in curling, and trying to change all that. But we don't get that without the Grand Slams coming first, which Martin had a huge hand in founding.

NIKLAS EDIN

Olympics: one gold medal (2022), one silver (2018), one bronze (2014)

Worlds: seven wins (2013, 2015, 2018, 2019, 2021, 2022, 2024), one silver (2017)

Europeans: seven wins (2009, 2012, 2014, 2015, 2016, 2017, 2019)

Grand Slam of Curling titles: four

Best team: 2016–present: Oskar Eriksson (third), Rasmus Wranå (second), Christoffer Sundgren (lead)

The evidence: The case for Niklas Edin is, well, his trophy case. It is simply fuller than anyone else's. He has an Olympic medal of every colour. He has the most World Championship wins of any skip, with seven, four more than the next closest (Glenn Howard and Randy Ferbey are tied with four each, though Ferbey has only three as a skip and Howard has just two). He also has more European titles than any other skip. In addition to that, he won both the Worlds and the Europeans four times in a row, which no one else has done. He is the only skip who has held the Olympic gold medal and the World title in the same year, when he won gold at both in 2022, just a few months apart. When it comes to winning at the big tournaments, no one has done more, especially considering you can also add a World Juniors and a World

University title to that heap of gold as well. Put simply: he is the only curler who could actually Scrooge McDuck with his medals, throwing them all in a pool and swimming with them. Well, he and his third, Oskar Eriksson, who could very well be put on this list as a sort of twin entry with Niklas. According to World Curling, each of them has won 33 recognized World Curling medals, of which 17 are gold.

The prosecution: As we said above, with international teams, there will always be one overarching question that remains achingly and painfully unanswerable: How good would their record be if they had to play in the Brier? Considering how Niklas has been close to or at the top of the World rankings for most of the last decade, and also considering how good he seems to be when the event is longer, it's fair to say he would have won a couple. But he has been to 13 World Championships. It is also very fair to say that if he and his team were Canadian, they would not have gotten to the Worlds that many times. Probably not even half as many times. As stated earlier, Brad Gushue holds the record for Brier wins as a skip, and he has six. He also got to his 20 Briers with the advantage of playing out of a weaker curling province in Newfoundland and Labrador. What if Niklas Edin lived in Alberta? Or Manitoba? He might only get to 10 or so Briers, and how many of those could he realistically win?[1] If Niklas Edin only goes to three or four Worlds, his record of seven wins is impossible to achieve. He also probably only goes to one Olympics in that period, maybe two. His Grand Slam record also leaves a lot to be desired.

Niklas himself has said that the shorter nature of Grand Slams, where you play four round-robin games instead of 10-plus, as you would at a Worlds or Olympics, does not suit his team as well as it does other teams. He has only four Grand Slam titles, and three of those came in the same season: 2016–17. Considering he has played in almost every Grand Slam since 2010, winning only four titles is quite low, and if you take away that 2016–17 season, he has won one title in 14 years. Most skips who have that longevity in the Slams have won more than four, and in quite a few cases, way more than four.

---

1 I decided to ask Niklas himself. His response: "Well, the humble thing would be to say that I might not have won any. Do I get to play out of a province where I'd go every year, like Brad Gushue?" I responded yes to this question. "Okay, then it's probably somewhere from three to eight. If I have to give you a number, we can split the difference and say five." He also put a smiley emoji in here, I think because he knew that number might upset Canadians. But he could very well be right. Even so, and even considering I'm bad at math, if you only go to the Worlds five times, you can't win it seven times.

For example, his European counterpart Bruce Mouat has only played in Slams regularly since 2017, and he's already won 10. All the other players on this list have won at least 10. Considering the Slams are often the sport's only representation of true best-on-best play, this is a problem when evaluating Niklas for GOAT status.

The defence: You can only do what is put in front of you. It's not Niklas's fault he is Swedish (in fact it's not anyone's fault that they're Swedish), and we don't have to answer any questions about how he might've done at the Brier, because he simply does not have to play in it. You could also turn the question around the other way: What if Canadian Team X was Swedish? In Sweden, the Worlds berth is sometimes selected by the national federation, and sometimes by a seven-game playoff. How many Canadian teams over the years had a better World ranking than Niklas Edin and might've been selected by Swedish Curling? How many teams might've beaten Niklas Edin in a seven-game playoff on club ice somewhere in Sweden? These questions are often unanswerable in two different directions, and this is no exception. Also, there have been lots of curlers from countries that aren't Canada who have made double-digit appearances at the Worlds. Andy Kapp from Germany went 14 times. John Shuster from the United States has gone 11 times. So has

Hugh Millikin from Australia. Pål Trulsen of Norway went nine. Do you know how many World titles they have, combined? That's right, it's zero. Just because you make it there year after year doesn't mean you automatically win. You still have to be good enough to do it. It's hard to win even one World title, never mind seven, and never mind four in a row. It's also plain to see that the Worlds are harder now than they have ever been, and that's not just a refrain for those who pine for the days of across-the-board Canadian domination. Sweden has always been competitive at the Worlds and sits at No. 2 on the all-time gold medal table, so the Worlds getting harder across the board also means something to them. And yet they have won more than any other team in this era, and continue to do so.

There's also the whole matter of the Olympics, which we are conveniently ignoring because it seems the Worlds is what gets yelled about more in curling lounges and on the internet. But again, we have teams that have been in as many Olympics as Niklas (four) and have no medals to show for it, or one medal. He has three, and one of them is gold. There have been seven male Olympic gold medallists ever. He is one of them. And as for the Slams? There is an argument to be had there, and Slam titles do mean a lot, but when you stack up the sheer number of Olympic and World successes against them, they don't seem to matter as much. If the number of Worlds and Olympic golds were closer to Martin and Gushue, then you could use Slams as a tiebreaker, but no curler will tell you a Slam title is more important than either of those, even if it is a great success to win.

So there you go. And now, like a brave boy, I will deliver the Verdict. What's that? I'm being told the judge is calling a surprise witness.

THE THIRD

When we think of the greatest players of all time, we are almost always thinking about skips. And sure, maybe they're like Kevin Koe or Glenn Howard, who had long stretches throwing third and eventually found their way to skipping, but their biggest moments are all as skips. There have been many great front-enders over the years: leads like Don Bartlett and Ben Hebert, seconds like Marc Kennedy (also a third) and Brent Laing and Scott Pfeifer, and many, many more. But I think that on the men's side of the game, there is one third who actually may have a case for being the GOAT.

JOHN MORRIS

Olympics: two golds (2010 in fours, 2018 in mixed doubles)

Brier: three wins (2008, 2009, 2015)

Worlds: one gold (2008), one silver (2009), one bronze (2015)

Grand Slam of Curling titles: 11

Best team: 2006–13: Kevin Martin (skip), Marc Kennedy (second), Ben Hebert (lead)

The evidence: The case starts with John Morris being the only man to have *two* Olympic gold medals. As for everything else, we can look back to Kevin Martin's case, and it's somewhat the same for John. He played on what I believe to be the best team of all time, and it was his decision to move down from skip to third that made it possible and unlocked a level in him (and Kevin Martin) they previously had not achieved. John made a Brier final as a skip in 2002, when he was just 23 years old, made it back to a Brier final as a skip (throwing third stones) in 2014, and made a legendary decision at the 2015 Brier to move himself from skip down to third and let Pat Simmons take the reins, which resulted in yet another Brier win for John. He also has a World title, is among the winningest players in Grand Slam history, and if you care about such things, also has back-to-back World Junior golds in an era before specialized teams, when they were very difficult to win.

The prosecution: As with Kevin Martin and Brad Gushue, we are talking about a single World title here. When compared with Niklas Edin's seven World titles, one title simply isn't a lot. Niklas also has three Olympic medals, which you will note is more than two. Two of them may not be gold, but he has three, and has a chance to add another in 2026, which John Morris will not since he is retired. Also, does mixed doubles count? I don't mean this sarcastically; I like the mixed doubles game a lot. But it's worth asking, for legacy. Obviously, it does in the sense that John has a gold medal in it, and that gold medal looks and feels the same as a four-person gold medal, but when we are discussing GOAT status, should mixed doubles even factor in? Most of the people in the GOAT conversation never even had the opportunity to play mixed doubles, or if they did, it wasn't at the Olympic level, where it has existed only since 2018. Winning a gold medal in mixed doubles is certainly impressive, but we can't rule out that it might not mean quite as much as single-gender four-person success, a version of the sport that has existed for centuries.

The defence: We haven't paid a ton of attention to "Brier finals" on this list, but John also has four silver medals to go along with the three golds, and one of those Brier finals (and an Olympic Trials final in the same year) was with Jim Cotter, who is certainly a good curler (and beat my ass many times at BC provincials) but never made the playoffs at a Brier or Olympic Trials as a skip without John calling the game and throwing third stones. Many people over the years have described John as the quintessential leader, and his work with Team Cotter seems to be pretty prime evidence of that. In fact, at the 2013 Olympic Trials, it was Morris himself who eliminated Kevin Martin in the semifinal. John made seven Brier finals in his career, and he did it with five different lineups. Most of the top curlers have had at least one constant: Niklas Edin has had Oskar Eriksson, Brad Gushue has had Mark Nichols, and Kevin Martin had Don Walchuk and then John Morris himself. For John to be involved in so many teams that had success is astounding and almost unheard-of for a back-end player.

From a leadership perspective, the mixed doubles gold medal is also quite impressive. Regardless of how you feel about mixed doubles, it speaks to his talent and ability that he won that tournament. You see, he had been working toward the Canadian Olympic mixed doubles team berth with Rachel Homan, who you will learn about in the women's GOAT chapter, up next. Many expected them to win or at least to be a *heavy* favourite heading into the Olympic Trials, but then Rachel won the Olympic berth with her four-person team and was unable to compete in mixed doubles, as per Curling Canada rules at the time. Morris needed to find a new partner, and fast, as the four-person trials were just weeks ahead of the mixed doubles trials in 2017. John called up Kaitlyn Lawes—who, make no mistake, is a phenomenal player with two Olympic golds and a very successful career—and they had one practice together, which they have said was only 30 minutes long, before heading to the trials. They started the trials 2–3, but then rattled off a bunch of wins and earned the right to represent Canada at the Olympics. Not many curlers would be able to come together so quickly, and on the grandest of the sport's stages, but John and Kaitlyn did.

And then, of course, as we've said, he was on one of the best teams ever, one so good that they won a lot of games by intimidation alone, and a big part of that intimidation was the fact Morris was playing third. In our game, usually, if someone has success as a skip—and John had it all, with the two World Juniors and a Brier final as skip—they stay a skip. His willingness to move down to third for one of the best skips of all time, in an era when back-end curlers typically just played their positions and shut up, made Team Martin so scary. It's almost like a baseball team building a lineup where you have two amazing hitters, one after the other. "What, if I pitch around him, I gotta face *him*?!" That's the way it was with John Morris and Kevin Martin, and so John Morris belongs in the GOAT conversation without having predominantly played skip.

THE VERDICT

Did I add a surprise witness just because I was afraid to write these next few sentences? I'll never tell. I am willing to bet, however, that if you polled curling fans as to which of these four players is the GOAT, the vote would be pretty split.[2] There's an excellent case for each of them. That said, I am going to have to choose Kevin Martin as my GOAT. I had one top player tell me they're not even sure it's close among these four. Although I tend to disagree there, I think it's hard to ignore what Kevin has done both on and off the ice for the sport and not put him at the top. Kevin is the closest person the sport has ever had to a universally recognizable name among the general population of Canada, and not just inside curling.[3] He has won everything there is to win in the sport, and while curlers may have a hard time deciding

---

2 I wrote this sentence and then thought, "Why don't I just do that?" A quick Instagram poll (very official) with over five hundred votes has revealed that the fans indeed are split: Kevin Martin 37 per cent, Niklas Edin 33 per cent, Brad Gushue 27 per cent, John Morris 3 per cent. A lot of pro curlers and analysts follow me (brag), and even their votes were pretty evenly split, with each curler receiving multiple votes from top players. John gets done a little dirty here, but at least two prominent former players with major titles in their trophy cases voted for him too.

3 Brad Gushue in Newfoundland and Labrador notwithstanding. Guy is a legitimate celebrity in that province.

who the individual GOAT is, a lot of them will tell you that the best team of all time was Martin's rink from 2008–10, which he led. Yes, Niklas Edin has more titles, and yes, so does Brad Gushue, but the total package remains Kevin Martin. Now, if Niklas or Brad could add another gold medal in 2026... Look, I'm already getting ahead of myself, but that's what makes the GOAT debate fun.

I'm sure that by writing this in a book that may be read decades from now, my take will age perfectly and everyone will always agree with me, and for that, I thank you.

CHAPTER 19

WHO IS THE GREATEST FEMALE CURLER OF ALL TIME?

It's probably true that one of the most spirited debates you can have in curling is about who the men's GOAT is. There are so many factors at play, as we saw, and we are in a situation where any of those four men could arguably be the GOAT. Fortunately, the women's GOAT debate is very cut-and-dried, and this chapter will be very short because everyone knows the correct answer. Just kidding!

The women's debate is very interesting for a few reasons: the debate about the top three (or four) contenders is a lot stiffer than the men's debate. I think most curlers would name one of the four men I offered as their GOAT, and there wouldn't be much debate about who the overall top five is. For the women? Hoo boy, that is much more complicated. And while there may be a seemingly clear No. 1, she is being hunted for her title by a curler who is still active and racking up wins at an unbelievable rate.

The women's GOAT conversation is also, sadly, a question of tragedy, and of how one player's career was cut short.

THE NARROW MISSES

As with the men, there will forever be a debate about how much a non-Canadian curler can be considered the GOAT, because they do not have to face down the gauntlet of the Scotties every season like the Canadian women do. That said, the gap at the World Championships is much narrower for the women than it is for the men, which suggests that overall, the Canadian women have not been as strong as the men have been against international competition. The men lead the World medal table with 36 golds, and the closest country is Sweden, with 12. For the women, Canada leads the medal table with 19 golds, and the closest is Switzerland, at 10. Granted, the women didn't have World Championships until 1979 (insane phrase to type), whereas the men started a full 20 years earlier (and Canada won 14 of those 20 golds), but still, the point stands. That said, with how many impressive European women there have been over the years, there are a lot more non-Canadians in the women's GOAT conversation. Here we go:

Connie Laliberte: Winning three Scotties out of the hardest province (Manitoba), winning a World medal of each colour, and coming second at an Olympic Trials, Laliberte is a curler who's run the gauntlet more times than most. She doesn't have the accolades that others on this list have, but is among the greatest Canadian skips.

Vera Pezer: Pezer is a tough name to properly rank because she played in an era when there was no Women's World Championship and no Olympics, but she won the Canadian championship (back when it was cringe-ily called the "Macdonald Lassies Championship") four out of five years in the late '60s and early '70s. She was also a stellar athlete off the ice, competing in two Canadian Senior Championships in golf and winning two national fast-pitch softball championships as well. That doesn't count for the purposes of this list, but you have to admit it is pretty cool.

Binia Feltscher: Two World golds, a European championship, and an Olympic silver. Her longevity doesn't stack up when compared with others on this list—even others from her own home country of Switzerland—but there were a few years when she was among the best in the world.

Mirjam Ott: Another Swiss player who had a lot of success, she won back-to-back Olympic silvers (one of which was while skipping Feltscher) and has a World title to go alongside. She was never the best player in the world at any point (her record in Grand Slams was poor), but two Olympic medals are more than most.

Kerri Einarson: Only two skips in history have won four Scotties in a row: Kerri Einarson and another skip coming up on the list. The issue for Kerri is that it hasn't translated to a single medal at the Worlds, and she has yet to make the Olympics for Canada either. Without either of those things, it's hard to put her much higher on this list, despite the fact she is in rarefied air when it comes to the Canadian national championships.

Dordi Nordby: Never the world's best player but one who always gave other curling nations fits, Norway's Nordby (say that 10 times fast) has a couple of World titles, a couple of European titles, and a couple of Olympic medals from the demonstration-sport days. She also has a whopping 11 World Championship medals and has a longevity some others don't, winning her first European Championship medal in 1983 and her last in 2004 (a year when she also lost the World final).

Elisabet Gustafson: One of the top players of the 1990s, Gustafson won a four-spot of both World and European championships (only Alina Pätz has won more), as well as a bronze medal at the debut Olympic Games in 1998. The only thing that holds her back from making the main list is that her run was relatively short and came in an era when the depth in women's curling was not great.

Anna Hasselborg: Hasselborg has an Olympic gold but doesn't have a World title, which unfortunately doesn't break her through to the next part of the list. She does have a World Mixed Doubles and a World Junior title, though, and an Olympic bronze too. The other thing Anna has going for her is that she's third all-time among skips for Grand Slam titles, with eight, and she won them all in the sport's most competitive era.

Cathy Overton-Clapham: Winner of five Scotties, "Cathy O" also has a World title and five other Scotties medals: one silver and four bronze. She also airlifted onto Chelsea Carey's team at the 2017 Olympic Trials and went all the way to the final there, despite having barely played with the team. In a field with so many good thirds, Cathy O is the best, but she doesn't have the Olympic success or the record as a skip to quite get there.

Eve Muirhead: Eve's resumé is among the best: a World Championship, an Olympic gold, an Olympic bronze, three European titles, and a World Mixed Doubles championship. She also holds the record for World Junior Championships, with four (three as a skip), and probably would've won a fifth if she hadn't had a scheduling conflict with the 2010 World Juniors, as she was playing in the Olympics for Scotland as a 20-year-old. No big deal, but she just doesn't have enough in her trophy case to be in the true GOAT convo.

Kaitlyn Lawes: Although she is a skip now, Lawes did most of her damage as a third, winning an Olympic gold and an Olympic title with a skip we'll see later on this list. She is one of only six people to have two Olympic gold medals, and the only Canadian woman to have two, as she also won the mixed doubles with John Morris in 2018. Her success as a skip in the last few years has been limited, and as a third she doesn't quite get into the upper echelon, but she's one of the best of this era.

Alina Pätz/Silvana Tirinzoni: I'm lumping these two together because even though Alina has two more Worlds than Silvana, so much of their success has been together, with Silvana calling the game and Alina throwing last. Alina has *six* World titles, but zero Olympic medals, not even a bronze, and that excludes her from the GOAT convo.

Colleen Jones: The female Glenn Howard, Colleen Jones is the toughest to leave off of this list, with a record *six* Scotties titles (tied with Jennifer Jones and several of her teammates) and two World titles, to go along with a World silver. She is the only skip other than Kerri Einarson to win four Scotties in a row, and she won five out of six from 1999 to 2004. She also had success in other categories, winning a Canadian and World Senior title, as well as two Canadian Mixed Championships. The lack of Olympic success holds her back from being in the GOAT convo, but boy, is she ever close.

THE TOP THREE

ANETTE NORBERG

Olympics: two gold medals (2006, 2010), one silver (1988, demonstration)

Worlds: three wins (2005, 2006, 2011), two silvers (2001, 2009)

Europeans: seven wins (1988, 2001, 2002, 2003, 2004, 2005, 2007)

Best team: 2003–10: Eva Lund (third), Cathrine Lindahl (second), Anna Le Moine (lead)

The evidence: There are six players in curling history who have two Olympic gold medals. Two of those players, John Morris and Kaitlyn Lawes, have one of those OGMs in a different category: mixed doubles. The other four? They are Anette Norberg and her team of Eva Lund, Cathrine Lindahl, and Anna Le Moine, who essentially ran women's curling from 2005 to 2010, winning several

World titles and both Olympic golds. Norberg is the only skip with two Olympic gold medals in the four-person discipline in either gender group. Norberg also holds the women's record for most World Curling–recognized medals, with 27. Much like Kevin Martin, both her individual excellence and the excellence of her team, easily one of the greatest of all time, vault her into this conversation. She also has the longevity factor, going to her first Olympics in 1988 and her last 22 years later, in 2010. And if that wasn't enough, after her three teammates retired, she took a team of players fresh out of juniors and with an average age of 23 to another World title in 2011. And just in case that somehow wasn't enough, she also starred in a power-metal music video for the band Hammerfall, which is extremely bad-ass.

The prosecution: We already went through this with Niklas Edin, but what holds true for any other European team also holds true for Team Norberg: How many World Championships and Olympics would they have gotten to if they were Canadian? For Norberg, the question is rendered at least somewhat moot because the Canadian Olympic Trials winner in both 2006 and 2010 was a team that was a bit of a shock winner, Shannon Kleibrink in 2006 and Cheryl Bernard in 2010, and Norberg beat Kleibrink in their only meeting at the 2006 Olympics, and she beat Bernard in the 2010 final to win gold. With

Norberg, there's also the very curious case of the 10-year blind spot on her record. She went to the 1988 Calgary Olympics and won the 1988 European Championships, and also appeared at the Worlds for Sweden in 1988, '89, and '91, winning bronze in all three years. And then... nothing. For 10 years. She does not make it back to the Worlds for Sweden for 10 full years, from 1991 to 2001. There is virtually no top curler in history, particularly a European one whose path to Worlds is putatively easier, who has a similar dry spell. Or, if there is, it's someone who isn't nearly as successful as Norberg would end up being. It isn't as though Norberg wasn't trying, either. She kept losing Swedish championships to Elisabet Gustafson, who won in seven out of those ten years and earned the right to represent Sweden at the 1998 and 2002 Olympics. Curling is a team sport, and maybe it's a case of finding the right team, but if Norberg were truly the GOAT, wouldn't she have had success regardless of roster makeup? And does the fact that she kept losing to the same player count as a strike against her dominance? It's worth asking the question, as a couple more World titles or some Olympic success in 1998 or 2002 would have cemented her case for GOAT even more.

The defence: Blind spot, shmind shmot. No other skip in all of curling has two Olympic gold medals. Her team from 2003 to 2010 is in the conversation for best team of all time, with their long run of success. Although it's hard to measure Norberg against her peers because she played before the Slam era, she had a long run of success against Canadian teams, and with so much of her run coming post–Colleen Jones and Jones's steady squad, she was probably the best team of the '00s decade, and the best skip. Any skip who can lay claim to a decade when they were the best team is in the conversation for GOAT. Not only that, but going to the Worlds in 2011 with a completely fresh team and winning again, defeating Canada in the final, is a feat in itself. That team was also young, and although they had been to the Worlds the year before, they were relatively inexperienced, and none of them would make the Worlds again, which makes it easier to make the case that in that era, Anette was the best skip in the world. On top of this, three may not seem like a lot of World Championships when you think of Niklas Edin's insane record of seven, or the fact that Alina Pätz has six, but there are only five last-rock throwers who have three World titles: Alina, Sandra Schmirler, Elisabet Gustafson, Anette, and the next player on this list. When you have the World Championship record she does and you add two Olympic golds on top of it, you are automatically in the GOAT conversation.

RACHEL HOMAN

Olympics: two appearances (2018, 2022)

Scotties: five wins (2013, 2014, 2017, 2024, 2025)

Worlds: three wins (2017, 2024, 2025), one silver (2014)

Grand Slam of Curling: 17 wins

Best team: 2022–present: Tracy Fleury (third), Emma Miskew (second), Sarah Wilkes (lead)

The evidence: Rachel Homan's resumé at age 36 speaks for itself. She continues to add accomplishments as of this writing, with a 2025 Scotties win on top of the four she has already won, and another World title that brings her World golds to three. She also holds the record for skips with 17 Grand Slam wins. She is technically tied with Jennifer Jones, but a few of Jen's wins were at events like the Autumn Gold and the Wayden Transportation Classic, which were considered "Slams" before women were officially at every GSOC event, but which, you could argue, don't hold the same weight. Rachel's longevity in the Slams also matters, as she won her first Slam in 2012 and her most recent one in late 2024. Of course, given how Rachel is now playing, it's likely she passes Jen's record (and may have passed it by the time you read this sentence) and extends her own Slam longevity streak. She is the only skip in the top three who can still add to her career resumé, and the fact that she's already in the GOAT conversation speaks volumes.

The prosecution: It starts and ends with the Olympics. Everyone else in the top three has at least one Olympic gold medal, and all their OGMs are remarkable in some way: Anette Norberg is the only one with two, Jennifer Jones is the only one to win hers while going undefeated, and Sandra Schmirler won the first one. After having two of the best seasons of women's curling any team has ever had, in 2015–16 and 2016–17, Rachel won the 2017 Canadian Olympic Trials and seemed destined for glory, entering the tournament as the defending World champion and the heavy favourite. And then she stumbled. She went 4–5, missing the playoffs and failing to put a cap on what was a tremendous run. She was able to return to the Olympics in 2022 with mixed doubles partner John Morris. Their team was selected under controversy, as COVID made it so that Curling Canada was unable to hold a mixed-doubles Trials, and had to hand-pick the team. They went with John and Rachel, and once again she fell short, as a 5–4 record was not good enough for the playoffs there either. Given how much of the sport now revolves around constructing teams to win the big prize at the Olympics, can a player truly be the GOAT with no Olympic success? Rachel will have more opportunities at the Olympics, but she's had two and not only doesn't have a medal but hasn't even been in a medal game. If her career ends this way, it will no doubt shape the overall conversation.

The defence: Most people would agree that regardless of the record, Rachel is probably the best pure shooter to have ever played, even if she retires tomorrow. No skip has made shots more consistently (and with a higher degree of difficulty) than Rachel has, and she has done it pretty much her entire career. Since she graduated from juniors, she's missed the Scotties only three times, and two of those were because she was playing at the Olympics. That's also playing out of one of the hardest provinces, Ontario. Curling Canada began to pre-qualify for teams for the Scotties championships as a way to combat certain provincial championships not being played owing to COVID. They then kept this rule, likely because of Rachel Homan, whose dominance in Ontario was such that keeping the rule made it so that women curlers in Ontario keep playing and aren't discouraged by the fact that Rachel will probably beat them in the final every year.

And how much do the Olympics really matter? It's one tournament every four years; just because Rachel hasn't been at her best there doesn't diminish what she's done for more than a decade at the highest levels of the sport. And this is to say nothing of the fact that her 2023–24 and 2024–25 seasons are two of the most dominant seasons ever in the sport, played with over a 90 per cent winning percentage (unheard-of) and winning four Slams and two Canadian and World titles in the process. And she's still only 36. There's a good chance she'll be able to play at three more Olympic Games. You have to have faith she'll get it done in one (or a few) of those. If she does and you're reading this book in 2035, she's already the GOAT and there's no debate. But for now, there still is, and that's because of...

JENNIFER JONES

Olympics: one gold medal (2014), one other appearance (2022)

Scotties: six wins (2005, 2008, 2009, 2010, 2015, 2018)

Worlds: two wins (2008, 2018), one silver (2015)

Grand Slam of Curling: 17 wins

Best team: 2010–18: Kaitlyn Lawes (third), Jill Officer (second), Dawn McEwen (lead)

The evidence: As with Niklas Edin, the case is, well, her trophy case. Jennifer Jones is simply the winningest skip ever. Although she doesn't hold the record for most World golds, her record at the Scotties is nearly unparalleled. Tied for the most wins, with six, she's also tied for second in consecutive tournament wins, taking three in a row, and she went to the Scotties a whopping 18 times and won a medal in 15 of the times she was there, which is a startling model of consistency. She also holds the record for most Scotties wins, with 157, a full 25 games ahead of second-place Colleen Jones, and Colleen played

12 more Scotties games than Jen did. This is to say nothing of the fact that to get to the Scotties, she was having to win the Manitoba title, one of the most (if not *the* most) competitive provinces to win. And saving the best for last, she is the only female skip to have won an Olympic medal undefeated, going 11–0 en route to the title and beating several GOAT candidates in the process there, including Eve Muirhead and Mirjam Ott. She's also the only Canadian female skip to represent Canada at the Games twice, doing so in 2014 and 2022.

The prosecution: Should the GOAT have more than two World Championships? It's a similar question to the one we asked about Kevin Martin in the last chapter, and it probably makes some sense to repeat here. There's always the caveat that winning a World Championship is harder for a Canadian team than it is for international teams, but even so, Jen gave herself six chances to win a World title, and only won a third of them, and made the final only half of the time. And considering that at least four of those World Championship appearances were in the "free bingo space" era of that tournament, you can make the argument that she probably should've won more. Yes, she was cursed by the horrendous ice at her first Worlds in 2005, and yes, there were great teams playing through her entire era, but given that she made it to 18 Scotties and six Worlds, the trophy case should perhaps be a bit fuller. She also made the Olympics twice, and in that second appearance, did not do as well as you'd expect, getting eliminated from the playoffs with a 5–4 record and losing to three of the four teams who finished above her in the standings.

The defence: The only female skip to go undefeated at an Olympics and win the gold medal. The defence could start and end there, as holding that record alone would get you at least an honourable mention for GOAT. When you consider all her other accomplishments on top of that, it makes for an easy case. Yes, she does only have two World titles, but the list of skips who have won multiple World titles is shorter than you think: Dordi Nordby, Sandra Schmirler, Elisabet Gustafson, Colleen Jones, Anette Norberg, Binia Feltscher, Silvana Tirinzoni, Rachel Homan. Only nine women ever have done it, and Jen is one of them. And you may notice that all of those skips are on this list as being in the GOAT conversation. So again, when you consider that *and* consider the Scotties record, the Grand Slam record, and everything else, the evidence is pretty overwhelming. And it's not just that, but also the longevity. Jen won her first Scotties in 2005 and was going to the Olympics as skip of Canada's best team 17 years later, in 2022. She retired last year, and you could easily make the case she didn't have to. When she decided to retire from curling at the 2024 Scotties, she did so off the strength of back-to-back runner-up finishes, losing to Kerri Einarson in 2023 and Rachel Homan in 2024. She also won her final Grand Slam title in her last season, 18 years after she won her first Players' Championship, in 2006. In short, she went out when she was close to being on top, a rarity in any sport. And not only that, she went out very close to being on top at the age of 49. Although people do think of curling as a sport you can play and play well into later life, Jennifer Jones is second only to Michelle Englot as the oldest skip to play in a Scotties final. She played the game at an exceptionally high level for a very long time, and her longevity at the top is almost unmatched.

As you may have noticed, there is one name glaringly missing from this conversation so far, and her success and career will always remain tough to quantify. But unlike John Morris, she is no surprise as a fourth GOAT contender.

GONE TOO SOON

SANDRA SCHMIRLER

Olympics: one gold medal (1998)

Scotties: three wins (1993, 1994, 1997)

Worlds: three wins (1993, 1994, 1997)

Best team: 1990–1999: Jan Betker (third), Marcia Gudereit (second), Joan McCusker (lead)

The evidence: Sandra Schmirler was as good as almost anyone in the pre–Grand Slam era, winning three Scotties (and medalling at a further two), winning the Worlds in all three of her attempts (in an era when Nordby and Gustafson were providing formidable opposition), and of course, winning the first Olympic gold medal for women at the 1998 Olympics in Nagano. It wasn't just that she won those championships, but that she also did so quite handily. In the three Scotties and three Worlds that she won, she lost a combined nine games. At the 1998 Olympics, she only lost one game. Seven tournaments against the world's best opposition, and she only lost 10 games. At the time, she was easily the best women's curler in the world, and was leading the GOAT conversation as soon as that gold medal was draped around her neck (overtop of those horrible Roots hats all the Canadians had to wear on the podium that year).

Unfortunately, just over a year after winning that gold, Sandra was diagnosed with what she called "the cancer from Mars," because doctors couldn't pin down exactly where the cancer came from. She was eventually diagnosed with metastatic adenocarcinoma, which rendered her unable to curl. Although she tried her best to continue commentating and involving herself in the curling world, the cancer was swift and brutal, and just six months after being diagnosed, she died in March 2000.

Her death so rocked the Canadian sporting world that her funeral was broadcast live on both TSN and CBC, who were home to the nation's curling coverage at the time. It was the first time a Canadian athlete's funeral was broadcast on two networks.

It doesn't feel right to do a prosecution and a defence in this case, but the impact that Sandra had on the curling world, and continues to have, is obvious, and it's easy to imagine that if she hadn't died at age 36, she would've continued adding medals to her trophy case and could easily have been the GOAT. As it stands, her legacy is the Sandra Schmirler Foundation, as I mentioned earlier, which helps babies who are born too small, too sick, or too far. It's one hell of a legacy to leave.

THE VERDICT

This one is closer now than it probably was a year or two ago. The men's is close too, but it does feel like there is some finality there because two of the GOAT candidates have careers that are over, and two of them are winding down. Their cases have (mostly) been made. And that's true of the women too, as only Rachel Homan is active among these four. However, Rachel is not only still active, but still relatively young at age 36, and she is currently the best player in the sport. She could have three more

Olympic runs in her, and could absolutely shatter the record books. Most curlers will tell you that Rachel is the most talented women's curler the world has ever seen, and that even if her trophy case doesn't currently match up, eventually, it will. I agree with that sentiment. I think Rachel is the best women's curler I've ever seen, and I think when it's all said and done, the GOAT conversation won't even *be* a conversation. Rachel will be on her own atop the summit.

That said, this book isn't being written in the future, and we have no idea what the future holds. Right now, Jennifer Jones has to be considered the GOAT. The undefeated Olympic gold medal is just too much for Rachel to overcome at the moment, especially considering that Rachel has made the Olympics twice and has not made the playoffs either time. The sport, whether fair or not, is now judged mainly on Olympic golds, and Rachel doesn't have one. I think her accomplishments are so strong that even if she never wins an OGM, but only, let's say, a bronze, she can still be called the GOAT. But she needs that medal. Jen was so good for so long, has the most decorated career, and has the one thing no one else who has ever played the sport does: an undefeated OGM. She was also tenacious, the best late-game player the sport has ever seen, who could make the hero shot or out-strategize you in a way that would leave you wondering

"How did we just lose?" And that undefeated OGM came on the heels of what is probably the most impressive single tournament we have ever seen from a player. Jen was absolutely dominant at those Games in Sochi, and right now, she is the GOAT of the women's game.

CHAPTER 20

THE FINAL END

We made it to the end. When I was just a junior curler coming up the ranks at the Peace Arch Curling Club and then losing basically every single big game I ever played in, I never thought that, eventually, I'd be able to write a book about the sport, and that people might actually want to read it. I am always hesitant when people ask me for advice about curling, because in some ways I don't feel equipped to give it. I never made it to the Brier. I certainly never got anywhere close to making it to a World Championships, or an Olympic Games. But I have played in thousands of curling games, I have been on the ice for tens of thousands of hours, and I've commentated, written, and produced content on the sport in some form for over a decade. And I *have* played in some big games: provincial finals, World Curling Tour finals. I mean, hell, I even made it to the semifinal of a Tier 2 Grand Slam once.[1] They aren't the biggest games, but they are big games, and that probably counts for something.

I wanted to spend the final chapter of this book reflecting on what the sport has meant to me, and what advice I could give as someone who has spent the better part of my life identifying as a curler,[2] to those who are still finding their way in the game. I know that this book might be read by some people who aren't curlers, but I still think that this advice will pertain to you no matter what you're pursuing, whether in a different sport or in something else entirely.

Weirdly enough, when you are a stand-up comedian, as I am, you get asked to perform at corporate events, and if you do that long enough, you may get asked to do a keynote. *Keynote* is just a fancy word for "a speech with a message," and you probably know that because you have been forced to sit in an uncomfortable, mass-produced hotel chair listening to someone in a suit drone on about synergy for one of the worst hours of your life. Just as I don't feel qualified to give curling advice, I don't feel

---

1 It was the only time I was ever in a curling tournament with Bruce Mouat, and my team finished ahead of his. I don't know much, but I do know that means I am officially better than Bruce Mouat. Sorry, dude.

2 My email address is *not* cullenthecurler@hotmail.com anymore, but maybe I'll bring it back.

qualified to do keynotes. Stand-up is way different, and I've never thought of myself as a keynote guy. But when I was asked by Curling Canada to give a keynote address to the field at the 2020 Canadian Junior Championships, I said yes.

I didn't really know what a keynote about curling would look like. I knew I had a few jokes I wanted to squeeze in there, but as far as advice went, particularly advice for curlers under the age of 20, I wasn't sure exactly what I wanted to say. Except for one thing. And that one thing has always come up for me over my years of playing and observing the game, and it's something I really believe is the most important thing you can do in curling. Don't worry, I did come up with more than one thing for that keynote, but I think one of the easiest and most confident pieces of advice I can give to you, my reader, and to anyone else who curls, is this:

Play with people you like.

It sounds very simple, and also very obvious and straightforward. But it isn't really, is it? Throughout your curling career, you are always going to be tempted by a very talented individual. Curling is a small-team sport, you have four (maybe five) members on your team, and that's it. In today's game, you need every member of your team to be good, and if they aren't, you can't go very far. Curling is also a skip's game. You need to play with a good skip or you'll also have very little chance of winning.

Maybe you yourself are the good skip. Congratulations. In that case, my advice to you is: "Don't be an asshole." That is also great advice for life in general, so you're welcome.

Throughout my career, I have seen people who are deeply unpleasant to be around find success in the sport because they are very good at it. But I have also seen many more of those same deeply unpleasant people eventually find themselves out of the sport because they couldn't find anyone to play with anymore. As I said, curling is a small-team sport, and chemistry plays a massive role in success. You can win games (maybe even big ones) without liking your teammates, but first of all, that is very hard, and second of all, that really isn't very much fun. The best success is shared success, and if you don't feel a kinship with your teammates, the wins will not feel as sweet.

I've interviewed many curlers over my time in the sport, and I'll always remember one part of one interview that has stuck with me for almost a decade now. My first attempt at a curling podcast, *Stone + Straw*, was based on the idea that curlers should be interviewed in person. At that point, there were some very good curling podcasts, but almost all of them relied on their guests being remote. Of course, that's fair: remote guests are much easier to book and schedule, especially in an increasingly global sport, but there is just no substitute for an in-person chat. With that in mind, I travelled across Canada to get interviews done for the pod. One of the places I went to was Sooke, BC, to talk to John Morris at his summer home. We sat on a dock overlooking the Pacific Ocean, and it was beautiful and tranquil and really everything you'd want in an interview. During that interview, I asked John about playing with Kevin Martin on what many feel was the best curling team of all time. The interview was taking place roughly 12 years after that team formed, and about five after it disbanded. As I outlined in the GOAT chapter, that team won it all: many Slams, multiple Briers, a World title, and an undefeated Olympic gold medal.

But John didn't really talk about that. I mean, he did, because I prompted him. But John left that team a year before it officially disbanded. Things got in the way of their success, and John left to play with Jim Cotter, while the remaining three members of Team Martin picked up Dave Nedohin. John told me he regretted leaving that team early, not only because they might have had a chance to win that 2013 Trials (John lost the final, after beating Kevin in the semifinal), but also because he robbed himself of another year of getting to be with those guys, who he called his best friends. He noted that the thing he missed the most wasn't the winning or the dominance, but rather the nightly card games they played together when they were on the road, enjoying a few whiskies and each other's company. He specifically said to me, "Those are the times you can never get back." Because if you're a good curler, the winning always feels achievable. John is retired now, but he went on to win Briers with other teams, and went to the Olympics again as a mixed doubles player. So the winning, you can get back. But the good times with your friends? That's what you can't.

If you ask most curlers, even at the highest levels of the game, to tell you a story about curling, 95 per cent of the time the first story they reach for is something that happened off the ice. It'll be within the curling world, of course—maybe something that happened at a bonspiel or in a curling club lounge or at a diner on the road. But almost always, it will not be something that happened during a game, or something that happened as the result of a win. It will be because they did something special, and they did it with their friends.

Not all of this wisdom is second-hand, by the way. I had a few years when I played with a skip who was extremely talented but who perhaps wasn't the greatest teammate. And we did have some success—we won a few World Curling Tour events, we won a bronze at provincials. It ended with a few broom-sized holes in the passenger door of my car because we had to kick him off the team in the middle of provincials for wanting to quit a game when we were only down three going into the ninth. When he turned up to our next game expecting to play, we told him he was off the team, and then he left the building. We went out and played the game (and won, as I recall), and afterwards my car had a few new accoutrements, shall we say. That at one point I had decided not to play with one of my best friends in order to play with this guy is something I genuinely still think about today. It's like a bad relationship, one you can't really see when you're in it. By the time it's over and you can reflect, you think, "Why did I end up there?" Fortunately, that friend agreed to come back and play with me the following season, and I had the most fun four years of my curling career playing with him and two other very great and very close friends (even if we did lose the provincial final twice).

Winning is great (I'm guessing—I've never done it), but the sport of curling is special because it isn't just about that. It's about the relationships you form with your own teams, with other teams, and with the greater curling community. So that's the advice I'd give to any curler, whether young or old. Play with people you like. If you don't, you may win, but you'll be missing out on the best things the sport has to offer. Curling has given me the opportunity to travel, to meet people from all over the world, and to have something in common with them right away. And it can offer that to people on a local level too. Just playing at your local club and meeting new folks from your own town or city you never otherwise would have met has its own rewards. It is a special sport, and what makes it special is the people, and the great part is, you have control over what you do. There is no owner telling you what the next step is, no GM who's trading for a player you hate and forcing you to get along with them; it's just up to you. And one of the easiest decisions you can make is simply to be around people you like, and to enjoy what this special sport has to offer.

Or you can read a book about it. I hear that's really great too.

ACKNOWLEDGEMENTS

First of all, this book simply would not have been possible without Charlie Demers, and not just because of his tremendous editing skills, which make my writing much better and much funnier. When I first pitched him the idea of writing a book about curling, five years ago, I never thought we would end up here. He not only encouraged me to write it, but offered the idea that there might be a home for it at Douglas & McIntyre, and made the connection to them for me. I don't have a literary agent, but I didn't need one, because Charlie knew the right people and knew that this book could eventually land where it did, even when I was positive that it couldn't. I also want to thank him for the nudge that we should pitch it again after the success of the *Broomgate* podcast. Without that nudge, I'd still be standing on the edge of the cliff, looking down.

Speaking of the *Broomgate* podcast, I would be remiss if I didn't mention that's a huge part of the reason why we are here, and I can't thank the team who worked on it enough. Chris Kelly, Pat Kelly, and Lauren Bercovitch at Kelly&Kelly for knowing and trusting that a podcast about curling would work in the same way a book about it might, and for being so unbelievably easy to work with. Kathleen Goldhar, our impeccable showrunner, who, in addition to being one hell of a journalist, will also be a life-long friend. Josh Bloch at USG Audio, whose direction and experience was invaluable. Mike Falbo, Brett Harris, and Ed Helms at Pacific Electric, who understood the vision of a comedy-adjacent podcast about curling immediately when others did not, and continue to work on its next life as a potential film and TV project. And, of course, the whole team at CBC Podcasts who helped push the show to No. 1 in our home and native land.

To Anna Comfort O'Keeffe and the entire team at Douglas & McIntyre, thank you for having faith in me and the sport of curling. I think curlers always worry that people won't take them or their sport seriously, but you did from the beginning and made this entire process so easy. You made it so that I never once thought I put this book in the wrong hands, and that means everything to me, so thank you.

Alyssa Hirose. Wow. I knew from the beginning I wanted illustrations to go along with this book, and I knew from the beginning I wanted to you to be the person to do them. Thank you for saying yes right away and for being as enthusiastic about this project as I was, even without knowing anything about curling going into it. Whenever I work with other artists, I like to put my trust in them, and trusting you with this project was easy. You didn't submit even a draft of an illustration I didn't like, and the book is so much better for your part in it, bringing to life my mad visions of Norwegian curlers walking a Paris Fashion Week runway. And to Aspen Allison, for the wonderful photo of myself that makes me look much more handsome than I actually am.

I've had a great many curling teammates over the years, and each of them was responsible for inspiring this book in some way, whether great or small (or by putting dents in my car). The four best years of my curling life were directly because of a great team that I had the privilege of being on. Not every curler is as lucky as I was to find a team of best friends to go into battle with, and that will never be lost on me. To Jay Wakefield, Paul Cseke, Dean Joanisse, and Brett Kury: in a lot of ways I owe my continuing love of this sport to you. Thank you.

When I was younger and ready to devour any content about curling, there weren't a great many curling books beyond strategy guides and player biographies. To Bob Weeks, Scott Russell, and Brian Chick, thank you for writing the curling books that gave me hope there might be a place in the world for another one.

To all the comedians I've shared the stage with, and to my podcast partners Bryan Quinby, Emily Heller, and especially Stefan Heck, thank you for inspiring me to be funny. Although writing a curling book is hard, writing a funny curling book is even harder, and it wouldn't have been possible without all the time I've spent cracking jokes with you all.

To my parents, John and Michele, thank you for always encouraging me to do whatever I wanted to do, even if that wasn't becoming an NHL player. I know you didn't always understand curling or why I loved it so much (and, quite frankly, still don't), but you were always there for me after a difficult loss or a big off-ice decision. To my dad, thanks for always allowing me the space to talk about my childhood and our relationship and for eventually understanding why I chose curling. And to my mom: I probably haven't helped you with your game enough, but the fact you took up curling 10 years ago and love doing it is one of the coolest things ever to me.

To my sister, Caitie: you're welcome for the fact that I quit hockey. You never had to get upset about me getting in a fight in a curling game. I know that sometimes being my younger sister wasn't (and isn't) always the easiest, but I know you're always there for me, and of course you know I will always be there for you. I'll also be there for your husband, Cole, and my wonderful nephews Beckett and Torrin, who, if I have my way, will become 10 times the curlers I ever was.

To my wife, Becca, who is the most gracious person I know. My career throughout most of our relationship has consisted of me telling you ideas I have out of the blue, and then you encouraging me to follow those ideas, even if it means time away from you or our relationship. I'll always be so grateful for your understanding about all the crazy and stupid things I do, and for never complaining about them, and especially for wanting to be the first person to celebrate the wins and offer comfort for the losses. There is no one else I'd rather come home to, and I love you the most.

To the rest of my family, the Cullens, the Quigleys, and the Priddles, thank you for always supporting my curling career, whether on the ice or off.

I messaged a lot of friends over the last few years, telling them I was making a podcast about curling and then telling them I was writing a book about it. Every single one of them thought that was cool, which was a refreshing change from my younger years, when I first started playing this nerdy game. I'm lucky to have many friends, and even luckier they are all encouraging. There's too many to list, but you know who you are, and I thank you.

And finally, to the curling world as a whole, from the players at the highest levels of the game to the curlers at my local club, to my fellow media members who cover this sport, to The Curling Group, thank you, thank you, thank you. I know it isn't always easy to hear your name on a podcast or see it written in a book, but you have all been so gracious with me and allowed me into your world, and it's a debt I can never repay. I promise to keep sticking up for this sport and I hope we continue, together, to bring it to a wider audience, because it really is the best sport in the world.

If you made it this far and you've never tried curling before, please do it. You won't regret it.

ABOUT THE AUTHOR

John Cullen has been a medal-winning semi-professional curler for more than twenty years. He has also worked as a teacher, writer, comedian and curling analyst, earning acclaim from such outlets as *Vulture*, *Forbes*, *The Economist* and *Esquire* for hosting the highly popular podcast *Broomgate: A Curling Scandal*. He has made televised appearances as a stand-up comedian and is a returning guest on CBC Radio's *The Debaters*. Cullen lives in Calgary, AB.